MSF, a

Delivering IT Solutions

Colofon

Title: MSF, a pocket guide

Authors:
Marlys Keeton Powers (lead author, Fox IT LLC, USA)
Jeff Carter (MSFmentor, USA)
Geof Lory (GTD Consulting, USA)
Andrew McMurray (Dimension Data, Australia)

Chief editor: Jan van Bon (Inform-IT, NL)

Review team:

Rolf Akker	(Inform-IT, NL)
Marco Ambrosoli	(Boston University, USA)
Arthur Coppens	(PinkRoccade, EMEA)
Holly Dyas	(Microsoft, USA)
Juergen Feldges	(Tireno Innovations, Germany)
Franz J. Hareter	(Skybow AG, Switzerland)
Paul Haynes	(Microsoft, USA)
Arnold Huebsch	(AMW, Austria)
Susan Joly	(Volt Technical Services, USA)
Christian Kolbeck	(Tireno Innovations, Germany)
Glenn LeClair	(Fujitsu Consulting, Canada)
Alex Lim	(I-Systems Consulting, Malaysia)
Simon Lingbeek	(Unisys, NL)
Ed Musters	(Systemgroup Management Services, Canada)
Vladimir Pavlov	(eLine Software, Ukraine)
Kathryn Pizzo	(Microsoft, USA)
Dave Pultorak	(Fox IT LLC, USA)
Pete Quagliariello	(Fox IT LLC, USA)
Andy Savvides	(Pictor Solutions, UK)
Saskia Schott	(SQLSOFT+, USA)
Rudi Stucki	(Zurich Financial Services, Switzerland)
Andrey Terekhov	(Microsoft, Russia)
Zuo Tianzu	(SinoServiceOne Ltd., China)

Paul Wilmot	(ManageOne, USA)
Lorraine Yu	(Microsoft, USA)
Jeff Yuhas	(Microsoft, USA)
Wim Zandbergen	(Unisys, NL)

Publisher: Van Haren Publishing (info@vanharen.net)

ISBN: 9077212167

Editions: First edition, first impression, January 2004
First edition, second impression, April 2006

Design & Layout: DTPresto Design & Layout, Zeewolde-NL

About this guide

This pocket guide is intended as a practical reference for information technology (IT) professionals studying or implementing Microsoft Solutions Framework (MSF). This guide is derived from and complements the core MSF documents, as described in chapter 14 of this guide.

The guide introduces the core components of MSF:

- MSF Team Model.
- MSF Process Model.
- MSF Disciplines.

Furthermore, the guide provides guidance on implementing MSF. Finally, the guide shows how MSF integrates with Microsoft Operations Framework (MOF). Both frameworks are complementary in Microsoft's approach to help organizations in delivering innovative solutions and achieving operational excellence.

Foreword

During these past 10 years, Information Technology (IT) has seen a dramatic increase in both its usage and the rate of change. Companies no longer view IT as a necessary overhead, but instead now recognize it as the key to future success. Businesses' demand on information is the driving force behind the need for IT solutions. Successful implementation of these solutions requires not only the technology but people and processes as well.

In today's climate, organizations are looking to processes and proven practices as ways to maximize their investment in IT. Microsoft recognizes this and created Microsoft Solutions Framework (MSF) to deliver on its 25 years of proven practices in software development and infrastructure deployment. Established in 1993, MSF was developed to enable customer and partner success in the implementation of IT solutions.

MSF focuses on the people and process sides of the IT equation. Through a series of models, disciplines and practices, MSF addresses roles, responsibilities, and processes within the project lifecycle. The flexibility of the framework allows each organization to easily adapt it to their own needs.

Microsoft would like to thank the customers and partners who have contributed to the on-going evolution of MSF.

Allison J. Robin
Director
Microsoft Solutions Framework
Microsoft Corporation

Contents

1. MSF Overview

Introduction

Microsoft® Solutions Framework (MSF) is a structured yet adaptable approach to managing technology projects, based on a defined set of principles, models, disciplines, key concepts, guidelines, and proven practices from Microsoft. It provides guidance on how to organize people and projects to plan, build, and deploy successful information technology (IT) solutions. MSF consistently focuses on the business value of the IT project by placing emphasis on delivery of the complete technology solution - all of the elements required to successfully respond to a customer's business problem or opportunity. MSF draws from a collection of internal and external best practices that have been proven effective in the management of all types of technology projects. Its easy-to-learn, easy-to-use, technology-independent approach makes it accessible to a wide range of organizations. Since its introduction in 1993, MSF has been used both nationally, and internationally, to successfully deliver technology solutions faster, with fewer people and less risk, while enabling higher quality results.

MSF's View of Solution Delivery

MSF concentrates on the three aspects of people, process, and technology involved in delivering solutions. Solutions include the coordinated delivery of technologies, documentation, training, and relevant components of service support and delivery, among others. MSF recognizes that no single structure or methodology is appropriate to all projects and environments given the wide variations in size, complexity, business requirements, and organizational and process maturity. It affirms that an adaptive approach is an absolute necessity for success.

MSF's philosophy for managing solution delivery is not to introduce a prescriptive methodology, but to provide a framework that is flexible, scalable, and technology-independent. In contrast to other more traditional project management approaches, its guidance is based on principles rather than rigid steps - this makes MSF broadly applicable. Whether the solution to be delivered is software development, infrastructure deployment, application integration, web applications, or a combination thereof, MSF components can be used individually or collectively to improve success rates.

In addition to its core principles, MSF uses two models, the Team Model and the Process Model, as the primary means for providing its guidance. The underpinning disciplines of MSF - Risk Management, Readiness Management (team knowledge, skills and abilities), and Project Management - are used extensively throughout the project life cycle to add depth and continuity. This multidimensional approach creates a solution delivery mechanism that extends end-to-end across development and deployment activities - from the initial project concept through implementation - to ensure business initiatives are well-understood and effectively integrated in the operational environment.

Why Microsoft Created MSF

Current environments have become increasingly more demanding of IT organizations: rapid change, increased consumer demands, new global markets and interdependencies, financial constraints, and an ever-widening and accelerating set of stakeholder expectations are the norm. Additional pressures come from within IT, where technological advances and constantly-changing work force must be factored into each project undertaking.

IT resources are increasingly under pressure to build within reduced schedules business-driven solutions that can be deployed and operated securely and cost-effectively. In the past, an IT failure could damage a company's operational ability; now it can threaten the bare existence of companies.

While new technologies have enabled many new business opportunities, technology projects continue to challenge IT. Many projects are unsuccessful because they are implemented with poor quality, excessive costs, or missed dates. Other projects squander precious resources through false starts, cancellations, or failure to implement. MSF was developed to help teams overcome the most common obstacles, thus improving business value, success rates, and solution quality.

Common Obstacle	What MSF provides to overcome
Poorly defined business problems or opportunities (and goals)	Establish clear, measurable project goals
Breakdowns in communication	Align business and technology goals using a shared vision and principles
	Focus on improving communication, within the team and externally
Unclear roles and responsibilities	Define and establish a set of easy to understand team roles and responsibilities
	Match resources (people and budget) to project needs, and resource needs to projects
Breakdowns in processes	Implement an iterative, milestone-driven process with clearly defined deliverables
Mistaken assumptions and unanticipated risks	Manage risk proactively using a well-defined approach
	Respond to change effectively and recognize its inevitability up-front

Table 1.1 Common obstacles in projects

IT organizations need to understand the businesses they support. Only by recognizing where that business is going, its goals and plans, can IT help the business be successful. MSF helps to forge a partnership between IT and the business. It lays the groundwork for greater understanding, accountability, collaboration, and communications.

Evolution of MSF

MSF has evolved over the last ten years and is now a robust and mature framework managed and developed by a dedicated product team within Microsoft. MSF originated from within Microsoft's own product development groups and from Microsoft Worldwide Services engagements, where it became integrated with well-known, industry-proven best practices. As MSF was developed and continues to evolve, these practices are consolidated and simplified for easier understanding and adoption, then verified through application in real-world projects. To stay abreast of the continually-changing and expanding needs of technology teams, Microsoft has looked to Worldwide Services, Microsoft product groups, Microsoft's internal operations and technology groups, Microsoft partners, and customers. Their successful experiences and practical innovations are incorporated into the development of MSF. An international advisory council of subject matter experts (SMEs) participates in MSF's development by providing guidance, reviews, and other input. Microsoft has found that involving outside expertise and experience helps to keep MSF up-to-date and relevant to what is happening in the industry and prevents it from becoming too parochial.

Thousands of people, internationally, have been trained in MSF and use it regularly. Teams use MSF within Microsoft to manage projects. Many Microsoft customers get their first introduction to MSF during engagements with Microsoft. These customers often adopt it and re-use it on subsequent projects as their preferred approach.

The most recent release of MSF, version 3.0, includes:

- *Updated Team and Process Models:*
  - The revised models provide a unified, adaptable framework with guidance for development, infrastructure, enterprise software integration projects, or other technology-based changes.
  - New Process Model phases. The Process Model now consists of five phases, combining the previously separate application development and infrastructure deployment models into one unified process for use in all types of projects.
- *Greater integration with industry standards* - Adding Project Management and Readiness Management Disciplines provides increased focus on building stronger, more effective teams. Refinements to the Risk Management Discipline extend MSF and add depth for broader application and improved scalability.
- *Linkages between MSF and MOF* - Connecting MSF and MOF ensures the close relationship of these approaches and helps project teams to deploy solutions into a production environment.
- *A new MSF Practitioner Program* - The new program has been created to ensure individuals have the knowledge and skills necessary to effectively lead an MSF project and/or participate as a project team member.

MSF Overview and Key Terminology

The basic MSF structure consists of eight core **MSF principles**, two **MSF models**, and three **MSF disciplines**. Although these components were designed to work together as an integrated whole, each component may be used individually as well. An organization might use their own project methodology, but adopt the core principles, or, it might use its own set of project roles, but use the five process phases. Augmenting the basic structure, **key concepts**, **proven practices**, and **recommendations** that apply to specific topic areas are used to extend MSF's applicability and adaptability on projects of varying size and complexity.

They are integrated into the models and disciplines.

To recap, the overall framework consists of:

- *Principles* - Microsoft uses the term 'Foundational Principles' for the core principles upon which the framework is based.
- *Models* - Schematic descriptions of principles, concepts, and proven practices that describe an entity or process. MSF includes two models, the Team Model and Process Model.
- *Disciplines* - Areas of practice using a specific set of methods, terms, and approaches (Risk Management, Readiness Management, and Project Management).
- *Key concepts* - Ideas that support MSF principles and disciplines and are displayed through specific proven practices.
- *Proven practices* - Practices that have been proven effective in technology projects under a variety of real-world conditions.
- *Recommendations* - Optional but suggested practices and guide-lines in the application of the models and disciplines.

Figure 1.1 shows how the MSF components are interrelated. The example begins with the MSF principle, *Learn from All Experiences*, which is employed in the MSF Process Model at key milestones. The successful application of the principle is dependent upon the key concept of *Willingness to Learn*, which is employed in the proj-ect through the proven practice of *Post-Milestone Reviews*.

The MSF recommendation for large and complex projects is to *Use External Facilitators* to maintain objectivity, ensure an environment that does not assign blame, and to maximize opportunities for learning.

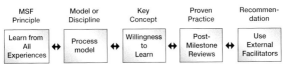

MSF Principle	Model or Discipline	Key Concept	Proven Practice	Recommendation
Learn from All Experiences	Process model	Willingness to Learn	Post-Milestone Reviews	Use External Facilitators

Figure 1.1 MSF Component Relationships

As indicated in the example, the framework is built around core principles that support decision-making and activities necessary for effective process and team collaboration. Principles unify the models and disciplines through a common set of values creating a flexible, adaptable structure. Within the models and disciplines, the principles are reflected in key concepts that are demonstrated through proven practices and the resulting recommendations.

The result is a solution delivery approach specifically designed to deal with changes, identify and manage risks, allocate resources, and establish easy to understand team and process structures.

The definition of several other key terms (table 1.2) is essential to comprehending MSF. Please consult the Abbreviations and Glossary chapter at the end of this guide for additional terms and definitions.

Customer	An individual or organization that expects to gain business value from the solution and is the recipient of a service or product.
Framework	A structure or frame designed to support something - it is assembled of component parts that integrate and fit together.
Milestone	A point on the project schedule at which the project team assesses progress and quality, and reviews deviations in scope and specifications. A project may use numerous milestones, external (or major) and internal (or interim).
Process	A coherent sequence of activities that yields a result, product, or service; usually a continuous operation. A series of actions or operations designed to achieve an end.
Project life cycle	A collection of generally sequential project phases whose name and number are controlled by the needs of the organization or organizations involved in the project.
Solution	Within MSF, the solution is the 'technical solution', the coordinated delivery of the elements needed to success-fully respond to a customer's business problem or oppor-tunity. A solution includes technologies, documentation, and training, as well as aspects of service support and delivery related to MOF (among others).
Sponsor	Individuals who initiate and approve a project and its results.
Stakeholder	A person with a significant interest in the outcome of a project.
User	The person who uses the solution or services on a day-to-day basis. Individuals or systems that directly interact with the solution.

Table 1.2 Key Terminology

MSF Principles

There are eight core principles upon which MSF is based.

The principles are tightly interwoven but also stand on their own merits in their applicability to projects of varying types, sizes, and complexity. Subsequent chapters will elaborate further on these principles and discuss how they are employed in their respective area.

1. *Focus on delivering business value* - Understanding why a project exists from a business perspective and how its business value will be measured is an essential element in delivering successful solutions. MSF teams understand how the project will satisfy the customer's specific business needs. The team understands the worth of the project to the business, which enables the team to maintain focus throughout the project.

2. *Foster open communications* - MSF endorses open communication that embraces team member, customer, and other key stakeholder input at all times. Individuals and teams need information to be effective. Team members, customers, and other key stakeholders must have confidence that information will be readily available and actively shared.

3. *Work toward a shared project vision* - The key enabler for MSF teams and processes is establishing a shared vision at the beginning of the project. In creating this vision, the team communicates to identify and resolve conflicts, and to clarify mistaken assumptions. This allows them to define the project's direction and goals in achievable, measurable terms.

4. *Establish clear accountability and shared responsibility* - All team members share overall responsibility for delivering a successful solution. In the Team Model, MSF defines clear accountabilities and responsibilities for each team role and their relationship to respective stakeholders. This is elaborated on in the Process Model.

5. *Empower team members* - Based on 'a team of peers' concept, MSF empowers team members by holding them accountable to

themselves and each other for the project's goals and deliverables. By accepting and sharing accountability and responsibility as equals, the team is empowered to make decisions, set direction, and take actions they deem necessary.

6. *Stay agile, expect change* - MSF takes the position that continuous change is expected and that technology solution delivery projects cannot be insulated from it. The iterative life cycle of the Process Model enables course adjustments to project activities and deliverables at progressive states of completion. It is supported by the Team Model where members participate in key decisions and respond to new challenges.

7. *Invest in quality* - MSF holds the entire team responsible for balancing the trade-offs of delivery, cost, and functionality to preserve solution quality and insulate it from compromise. Team members must build quality into each of their deliverables for the completed solution to be successful and IT organizations must invest in their team members (through education, training, and experience).

8. *Learn from all experiences* - The last twenty years have witnessed only marginal increases in technology project success rates. Given that the major causes of failure are primarily the same, IT organizations do not appear to be learning from their unsuccessful projects. MSF embraces the concept that continuous improvement based on individual and team learning will lead to greater successes.

MSF Models: Team and Process

MSF contains two models: the Team Model and the Process Model. The purpose of the **Team Model** is to enable project scalability and to ensure teams meet various stakeholder needs through its definition and assignment of goal-driven roles and responsibilities. The Team Model identifies who does the work during the project and links each team role with a major project responsibility.

The purpose of the **Process Model** is to drive fast, high-quality results through a proven project life cycle using a key set of project activities and deliverables. The Process Model works in conjunction with the Team Model by organizing the process into distinct phases and milestones for creating, testing, and deploying a solution.

MSF Disciplines: Risk Management, Readiness Management, and Project Management

Disciplines are necessary throughout the life cycle of the project and are constant guides for each of the models. MSF relies on three disciplines: the Risk Management Discipline, Readiness Management Discipline, and Project Management Discipline.

The **Risk Management Discipline** is a comprehensive, proactive approach to increase the likelihood of project success by minimizing the negative factors that could impact project success. Risk Management reduces surprises and expensive 'fire-fighting' activities by providing guidance for proactively managing project risks.

The **Readiness Management Discipline** helps project teams identify skill gaps and opportunities for learning. Readiness Management proactively identifies the skills required by the team matching resources to project needs and schedule requirements. Use of Readiness Management enhances individual skill sets as projects provide opportunities for learning and growth.

The **Project Management Discipline** applies industry-standard project management best practices to MSF principles. By streamlining project management activities, the Project Management Discipline helps the team be successful rather than hindering its performance with additional overhead that may not provide sufficient value for the resource investment.

MSF and MOF/ITIL

Any discussion of MSF would not be complete without examining its relationship to Microsoft Operations Framework (MOF). MOF is Microsoft's structured approach for helping customers achieve excellence in managing operations. As with MSF, MOF provides a collection of principles, models, and guidance. MOF is Microsoft's adaptation of the international standard for IT service management, the Information Technology Infrastructure Library (ITIL).

MOF focuses on service support and delivery with the goal of achieving high reliability, availability, security, and manageability on mission-critical production systems. Microsoft Solutions Framework focuses on solution delivery, namely the envisioning, development and deployment of technology and related elements in response to a business need. These two slogans summarize the goals of MSF and MOF:

MSF = Build IT right.
MOF = Run IT right.

MSF and MOF are complementary frameworks. IT organizations use MSF to develop and deploy solutions and use MOF to operate and manage those solutions on an on-going basis. While MSF guides the planning, building, and initial deployment of solutions, MOF facilitates the implementation, management, support, and evaluation of the solution in the production environment.

MSF and MOF have been designed to work well together, as well as independently. MSF is all about technology solutions and takes the solutions perspective. MOF is based on MSF and takes the operations perspective. MOF is about service support and delivery capabilities - service solutions - that operations provides to the business. Both MSF and MOF provide a view of the IT life cycle and incorporate an enterprise and a systems perspective for their planning and deployment activities, as reflected in figure 1.2.

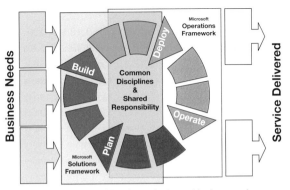

Figure 1.2 How MSF and MOF work together to meet business needs

Within the overall IT life cycle, MSF and MOF follow four basic steps to create a new solution (or change to an existing one) and to operate that solution in a production environment. These are:

1. *Plan a solution using MSF* - Understand the business and operational requirements in order to create the solution architecture, design, project plans, schedules and so on.
2. *Build a solution using MSF* - Complete the features, components, and other elements described in the specifications and plans.
3. *Deploy a solution using MSF & MOF* - Effect a smooth transition into the production environment.
4. *Operate the solution using MOF* - Use the MOF models and processes to achieve and maintain operational efficiency.

In addition to these shared perspectives, the three disciplines (Risk, Readiness, and Project Management) can be applied to both solutions delivery and operations. IT organizations that employ both MSF and MOF guidelines (Principles, Models, and Processes) will develop a broader perspective for effective solution delivery as well as for excellence in support and operations. This will also serve to create greater awareness of the best way to meet project and service management expectations without decrementing or disrupting services. Throughout the IT project life cycle, the MSF team can make decisions that result in greater overall satisfaction and fewer surprises by examining impacts to and requirements from Service Management Functions (SMFs) within MOF's Optimizing Quadrant, see table 1.3.

Service Level Management	Service Continuity Management
Capacity Management	Financial Management
Availability Management	Workforce Management
Security Management	Infrastructure Engineering

Table 1.3 Related SMFs in MOF's Optimizing Quadrant

Additionally, MSF intersects with MOF's Changing Quadrant where, during the Envisioning Phase, MSF project plans and schedules are synchronized with Release and Change Management activities to provide more effective planning for the IT environment. MOF Configuration Management can be used to help identify impacts and interdependencies as MSF requirements and functional specifications are developed. Conversely, MSF can be useful to operations groups as they undertake project-based work (for example, changes, maintenance projects, and so on). The combination of these two frameworks makes a powerful contribution to improving how solutions are delivered and how the systems for those solutions are run.

2. The MSF Team Model

Overview

The MSF Team Model defines the roles and responsibilities of a team of peers working in interdependent, multidisciplinary roles. All project work is performed by individuals who must work together toward a common goal while representing their individual identities and unique perspectives. The MSF Team Model is based on the concept of cross-functional teams representing the different points of view, with all team members behaving as peers and collectively managing the outcomes. Figure 2.1 is a logical depiction of the MSF Team Model.

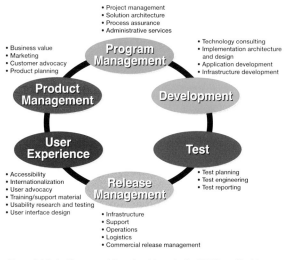

Figure 2.1 Role Clusters and Functional Areas in the MSF Team Model

The MSF Team Model is based on the premise that any technology project must achieve certain key performance goals in order to be considered successful. These goals drive the team and define the Team Model. The MSF Team Model emphasizes the importance of aligning role clusters, also referred to as roles, to areas of responsibility, each of which requires a different discipline and focus, as well as performance competencies.

Since each goal is critical to the success of a project, the roles that represent these goals are seen as peers with equal say in relevant decisions. The absence of any role increases risk and jeopardizes the success of the project. The associated performance goals and roles are shown in table 2.1.

Key Performance Goal	MSF Team Role Cluster
Satisfied customers	Product Management
Delivery within project constraints	Program Management
Delivery to product specifications	Development
Release after addressing all known issues	Test
Smooth deployment and on-going management	Release Management
Enhanced user effectiveness	User Experience

Table 2.1 MSF Team Model and Key Performance Goals

Guidelines for the functioning of the MSF Team Model, as well as its structure, are organized around the preceding performance goals. Note that one role is not the same as one person - a person may take on more than one role, or multiple people can take on a single role. The MSF Team Model further defines how this combination of roles can be used, based on the associated risk, to scale up to support large projects with large numbers of people or scale down to support projects that have a small number of people in a single team through the combination or sharing of roles.

The MSF Team Model is perhaps the most unique aspect of MSF. At its heart is the fact that technology projects must reconcile the disparate and often interrelated needs and goals of various stakeholders. The MSF Team Model fosters this melding of diverse ideas, thus recognizing that technology projects are not exclusively an IT effort.

The MSF Team Model represents the compilation of industry best practices for empowered teamwork. When applied within the MSF Process Model they can outline activities and create specific deliverables to be produced by the team. These primary performance goals both define and drive the team. Combined, the Team and Process Models help define who does what and when to produce what.

A detailed discussion of each role cluster and its functional responsibilities follows.

Product Management Role Cluster

The key goal of the Product Management role cluster is satisfied customers, those who will receive the business value of the solution. Projects must meet the needs of customers in order to be successful. Product Management represents the interests of the customer to the project team. To satisfy customers, the Product Management role cluster must adequately address the functional areas of product planning, business value, customer advocacy, and marketing.

Functional Responsibilities of Product Management

Functional responsibilities of Product Management include the following tasks:

- Drives product planning by articulating and prioritizing customer and business requirements through market research and competitive intelligence/analysis.
- Drives marketing and public relations messages that address the target customer and differentiates the solution from that of the competition.
- Provides the business value by defining, measuring and maintaining the business justification and success criteria for the project.
- As the customer advocate, drives a shared project and solution vision while managing customer expectations and communications.

Program Management Role Cluster

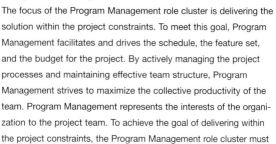

The focus of the Program Management role cluster is delivering the solution within the project constraints. To meet this goal, Program Management facilitates and drives the schedule, the feature set, and the budget for the project. By actively managing the project processes and maintaining effective team structure, Program Management strives to maximize the collective productivity of the team. Program Management represents the interests of the organization to the project team. To achieve the goal of delivering within the project constraints, the Program Management role cluster must adequately perform the functional areas of project management, process assurance, administrative services and solution architecture.

Functional Responsibilities of Program Management

Functional responsibilities of Program Management include the following tasks:

- Performs the administrative responsibilities of tracking, managing and reporting on the master project schedule and budget.
- Implements project management processes including managing Change, Risk and Readiness Management Disciplines, and supports the team leads in using them.
- Facilitates communication and the collaborative development of the overall solution design by assuring consensus on the solution scope, functional specification, and critical trade-off decisions.
- Drives productivity and process quality assurance through reviews and recommends improvements.

Development Role Cluster

The focus of the Development role is building the solution to the specification. To succeed in meeting this performance goal, the Development role must build a solution that meets the customer's expectations as expressed by the team through documented specifications. Development serves the team as the technology consultant and solution builder. As builders, the Development role provides solution and feature design, estimates the effort required to deliver that design, and then builds and documents the solution.

Functional Responsibilities of Development

Functional responsibilities of Development include the following tasks:

- Serves the team as a technology consultant by evaluating and validating technologies.
- Participates actively in the creation and review of the functional specification
- Develops the solution features to meet the design specifications and performs unit testing as defined in the test plan with the support of the Test role.
- Supports product stabilization by fixing bugs and preparing the product for deployment.

Test Role Cluster

The focus of the Test role is to assure that all issues regarding the quality of the solution have been identified and addressed. This is a continuous effort throughout the project as each deliverable is 'tested' for its quality relative to the agreed-upon quality bar. Every solution will have some deficiencies, and it is the Test role that brings these to the forefront and drives resolution. The Test role represents the agreed upon quality bar to the team. To be successful, the Test role cluster must focus on the key responsibilities of test planning, test engineering, and test reporting.

Functional Responsibilities of Test

Functional responsibilities of Test include the following tasks:

- Develops the testing approach, plan, and specifications, which will identify and set the quality bar for the solution.
- Develops and maintains automated test cases, tools, and scripts,

and conducts tests to accurately determine the status of the solution.

- Provides the team with data related to product quality by reporting on the test results and solution status.
- Tracks all bugs and communicates issues to ensure their resolution before solution release.

Release Management Role Cluster

The goal of the Release Management role is to assure smooth deployment and transition to effective on-going operations. As such, Release Management acts as the primary advocate between the project team and the operations groups. As the representative of those who will own the solution in production, Release Management is a key link between the roles and processes of MSF and those of MOF that govern a project. In order to achieve its goal of smooth deployment and effective on-going operations, Release Management focuses on infrastructure, support, operations, logistics, and solution release or configuration management.

Functional Responsibilities of the Release Management Role Cluster

Functional responsibilities of Release Management include the following tasks:

- Supports the business by managing the service level agreements (SLAs) with the customer and ensuring commitments are met.
- Drives and sets up support for pilot deployment by building test and staging environments that accurately mirror production environments.
- Prepares operations through physical environment use and planning, training, and adherence to operational standards.
- Coordinates commercial release elements such as packaging, product registration, licensing management, channel management and distribution.

User Experience Role Cluster

The focus of the user experience role is enhancing user effectiveness. The user experience role represents those who will have direct contact with and use of the solution, which may or may not be the same as the customer or sponsor. This role can be extremely challenging because it takes a wide range of skills to assure that the diverse needs and interests of such a broad constituency are adequately represented in the solution. To assure that user effectiveness is enhanced, this role focuses on accessibility, internationalization, user advocacy, training and/or support, usability research and testing, and user interface design.

Functional Responsibilities of User Experience

Functional responsibilities of User Experience include the following tasks:
- Gathers, analyzes, and prioritizes user requirements and provides feedback and input to solution design through usage scenarios and/or use cases.
- Drives user interface design.
- Designs and develops documentation for support systems (Help Desk manuals, Knowledge Base articles, and help files).
- Develops and executes user learning and readiness strategy.

Team Model Principles

The Team Model is at the same time both the most difficult and most beneficial element of MSF any organization can adopt. The decision to change the management and team processes should not be taken lightly. Before undertaking this challenge, it is essential to understand the underlying principles of the Team Model and assure they are consistent with the professed or desired values of the organization.

At the heart of the MSF Team Model are six of the core principles. If the six principles were integrated into the everyday behaviors of team members, the team of peers would almost happen by itself. Therefore, to implement the Team Model, begin with the following principles:

- *Focus on delivering business value* - The MSF Team Model has representation from three business perspectives unrelated to development - the customer, the user, and operations.
- *Foster open communications* - Given the diversity of roles and focus, open communication is essential to achieving a shared vision.
- *Work toward a shared project vision* - The diversity of the team of peers, even with open communication, will quickly diverge if not held together by a common vision.
- *Establish clear accountability and shared responsibility* - Combined with a shared vision, the individual roles are driven to fulfill their role through clear accountability and shared project responsibility.
- *Empower team members* - Team members need to feel individually and organizationally empowered to exercise the necessary autonomy and fulfill their commitments.
- *Stay agile and expect change* - The MSF Team Model fosters the agility needed to address new challenges by involving all team roles in key decisions, thus ensuring that issues are explored and reviewed from all critical perspectives.

By integrating these principles into team processes, the power of the team will be seen through increased productivity, greater creativity, higher morale, and unmatched quality of deliverables. One of the benefits of the principle-based nature of the MSF Team Model is that it can be adopted in part or in whole and still provide tremendous value.

Through guidance and practice, the disciplines can be developed and exercised within the models to effectively create the proven practices that will become the instantiation of the framework within the organization. This bottom up (or inside out) approach has proven to be the most successful way to create sustainable change. Successful application of MSF starts with understanding and adopting MSF's principles at both an individual and a team level.

Scaling the Team Model

The MSF Team Model advocates breaking down large teams (those greater than ten people) into small teams working in parallel, with frequent opportunities to synchronize their efforts. This is accomplished through the creation of either function or feature teams. Feature teams are smaller sub teams that organize one or more members from each role into a matrix organization. These teams create a particular feature set or outcome, and are responsible for all aspects of it, including its design, schedule, and delivery.

Function teams are teams that exist within a role, where each member of the function team is focused on the performance goal of that role. Within that function team, each person will perform some subset of the overall role functions. Feature and function teams are usually represented to the larger team through a team lead to expedite communications. Through the construction of feature and/or function teams, it is possible to create large teams that are unencumbered by the bureaucracy that often hampers traditional hierarchical teams.

Even though the Team Model consists of six roles, a team can be any size as long as someone can adequately represent each of the six goals necessary for success. Typically, having at least one person per role helps to ensure that someone will represent the interests of each role. However, on smaller teams, roles must be shared across the team membership. When sharing roles, it is risky to combine roles that have intrinsic conflicts of interest, represent opposing constituencies, or require extremely different skills.

Tips and Considerations for Implementing the MSF Team Model

There are no shortcuts to implementing the MSF Team Model. It requires building individual and collective skills and disciplines, which takes time and effort. Through years of experience, Microsoft can provide the following field-proven tips and considerations to encourage adoption:

- Set up a safe environment where teams are allowed to exercise their new behaviors without fear of failure or retribution.
- Use collaboratively developed deliverables to allow team members to practice open communications, develop a common purpose, and feel empowered.
- Include representatives from the business and from operations to fill the roles of Product Management, User Experience, and Release Management.
- Create a clear and well-communicated team structure so that everyone knows who is focused on what and who their constituents are. Team structure should also define team processes for items such as change control, problem resolution, and decision-making.
- Try not to combine roles that have intrinsic conflicts of interest. For example, separate the three roles of Product Management, Program Management, and Development, and resist the temptation to combine the Program Management role with either of these other two roles. Separate Development and Test.

Overview

The MSF Process Model establishes a series of tasks, assembled into five distinct sections, or 'phases'. The description of each phase includes the necessary activities to deliver a project from inception to final delivery and sign-off by the customer. The five phases use the concepts of milestones and deliverables as points that represent distinct achievement as well as opportunities for reflection during the life cycle of the project, as shown in figure 3.1. The phases are named after the activities that drive them, and each has a distinct mission, shown in table 3.1.

Phase Name	Mission
Envisioning	Define project goals and expectations
Planning	Define what needs to be built, timeline, and procedures
Developing	Build, test, and refine all aspects of the solution
Stabilizing	Test solution and prepare for final release to production
Deploying	Deploy solution into live production environment

Table 3.1 Five Phases

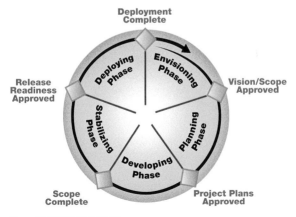

Figure 3.1 MSF Process Model

The Process Model combines the strengths of two well-known models used in traditional software development, waterfall and spiral:

- *Waterfall* - Uses an unchanging set of project conditions with a series of inflexible milestones to produce distinct sets of tasks and schedules that represent transition and check points of the project.
- *Spiral* - Uses a continually evolving idea of the solution, which allows greater scope for change. Due to a lack of clear goals, many spiral-based projects can suffer from expanding deadlines and excessive costs.

This produces a model that is both prescriptive in its clear delineation of progress points and delivery of goals, but is also flexible enough to accommodate changes in project direction. Through milestones, reviews of deliverables, and approvals, the team produces discrete items that represent advancement to the team and stakeholders of the project. The internal post-milestone review, meanwhile, is used to evaluate the project in a customer-free environment. The phases of the Process Model are not a fixed structure and can overlap; for example, certain development duties can be carried out as the Stabilizing Phase is beginning.

Milestones, Deliverables, Reviews and Approvals

Milestones are a crucial component of MSF because they mark identifiable achievements of the project. At these milestones, the deliverables are presented to the customer and other key stakeholders, progress of the project is monitored, and suggestions made as the project transitions into the next major phase.

Milestones are broken down into two types: major and interim. Major milestones represent the culmination of Process Model phases and serve as transition points, while Interim Milestones are generally internal phase progress points for synchronization. Without these milestones, it is difficult for the team to remain focused on project tasks. This can result in missed deadlines and excessive costs. In addition, the customer can lose confidence in the project team's ability to effectively deliver the needed business solution.

The major milestone is a transition point for responsibility of the project to other roles. Each phase is characterized by 'ownership' from one or more of the team roles. The phase-owner is responsible for overall guidance of the project through to the next major milestone. Although Program Management can be seen as having overall responsibility for the project schedule, each phase's milestone and associated owner can be seen in table 3.2.

Milestone	Responsible Role Cluster
Vision/Scope Approved	Product Management
Project Plans Approved	Program Management
Scope Complete	Development and User Experience
Release Readiness Approved	Test and Release Management
Deployment Complete	Release Management

Table 3.2 Milestones

Each major milestone is also the point for affirming customer and other key stakeholder approval through sign-off of the work to date. This leads to permission to move to the next phase, which occurs during the milestone review meeting. After approval is gained for transition, the team will hold a post-milestone review, providing an internal forum to determine what went right, what went wrong, and what can be improved for the next phase of the project. Deliverables for the first two phases are foundational and are discussed in greater detail than others.

Iterative Approach

As mentioned earlier, the MSF Process Model is a hybrid of two common models, the waterfall and spiral. MSF takes the concepts of milestones within the waterfall model to evaluate progress, and uses the iterative, evolutionary nature of the spiral to produce a model with clear points of progression, combined with adaptability. MSF sees the Process Model as an iterative approach to development and implementation. It is recognized that an attempt to build every possible feature into a solution will cause several risks, namely:

- Prohibitive costs.
- Delivery delays.
- Delays in delivering business value.

MSF advocates versioned releases to provide core functionality as quickly as possible followed by a number of later releases that add desired functionality. This ensures that the business benefits are realized quickly. It breaks down the solution into manageable, prioritized units, which can also become smaller, separate projects in themselves. The number of iterations for the project must be agreed upon by the customer and represents a phased approach to fulfilling all requested features for the solution. This may take the form of a fixed number of projects to deliver functionality or may follow a more open-ended approach.

The iterative approach also allows for the creation of 'living documents', continually reviewed and updated throughout the course of the project, beginning during the Envisioning Phase with the vision/scope document. These documents will be refined further during subsequent phases until the team deems it is time to freeze the feature set of the solution (i.e. the point in time where changes are no longer permitted). This is unlike the waterfall method, which forces the team to adopt a set of features early in the development process - features that cannot be changed as the project continues. The Process Model's mature approach accepts that requirements must and will change during the life cycle of the project.

Process Model Principles

As previously mentioned, certain MSF principles are used throughout the Process Model:

- *Focus on business value* - The solution provided by the project must satisfy some distinct business need and be deployed into a production environment to be effective. To reflect this, the MSF Process Model devotes a phase to deployment, which also transitions into MOF for continuing support after the project life cycle has officially ended. This principle is also useful during the Developing Phase, since the process of tracing all work back to a business need helps to focus development toward needed functionality and guards against scope creep.

- *Foster open communications* - The Process Model promotes open and effective communication that embraces team member and customer input at all times. This contributes to project success. The combination of frequent (milestone) reviews and written project deliverables ensures that, at all times, the state of the project is clearly visible to all team members and customers involved.

- *Work toward a shared project vision* - If the project is to succeed, it is absolutely imperative that all team members and customers have an understanding of what the project is trying to achieve. The need for communicating and creating a unified project vision for the team and the customer is considered so important that the first phase of the Process Model dedicates its major milestone and deliverable to achieving this vision.

- *Stay agile, expect changes* - Because MSF accepts and embraces the idea that there will always be a certain amount of change, solutions are baselined early in the Planning Phase and generally not frozen until the final stages of development; changes in scope can be addressed without great hardship.

- *Empower team members* - MSF gives opportunities for team members to take ownership of aspects of a project and allows them to make decisions related to those areas. This stimulates team members to be aware of the value and importance of their input to the project.

- *Establish clear accountability, shared responsibility* - Role clusters have distinct areas of accountability and responsibility for their areas of the project to help convey a sense of ownership toward all aspects of their cluster.

Key Concepts and Proven Practices

The following concepts and practices are crucial to the Process Model:

- *Use change control procedures* - By using change control procedures, the process ensures that any changes to the base-lined scope are not arbitrarily added. Each change should be examined for possible impact to the project. Any change to the scope of the solution should be documented and circulated to all involved for approval before implementation.

- *Manage trade-offs effectively* - All projects will at some point face a trade-off decision between the variables of resources, sched-ule, and features. Change to any of these elements will cause another to change in reaction. The relationships between the three variables are visualized by the trade-off triangle and trade-off matrix, as figure 3.2 illustrates.

  Here it can be seen that choosing one of the variables as being 'fixed' will require a corresponding prioritization of another, which in turn will lead to constraints for the final variable. For instance, in a project to create a purchasing system, it is decided that the project must be done in three months, that the desired features are as listed, and therefore, that the resources that must be allo-cated can be obtained, given those parameters. In this case, if the customer were to choose a long-term schedule, the feature set could be adjusted to include more functionality than if the schedule was set to an earlier ship date.

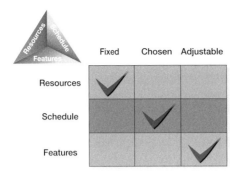

	Fixed	Chosen	Adjustable
Resources	✔		
Schedule		✔	
Features			✔

Figure 3.2 Trade-off Triangle and Trade-off Matrix

- *Baseline early/freeze late* - Creating a baseline as early as possible in the project allows the development team to have a clear sense of direction, thus allowing them to begin work quickly. Allowing the solution to remain dynamic for as long as possible and freezing late in the development process ensures that a change in business needs can often be incorporated into the final release.
- *Utilize a multiple-release plan* - Aim to provide additional low-priority functionality in future releases of the product to control scope creep, while providing the capability to respond to changing customer needs.
- *Schedule for an uncertain future* - Assume that the project will experience unforeseen delays, and add a reasonable amount of buffer time to compensate. The decision to include buffer time rests with Program Management; this will not be added into the schedule at each stage. Rather, buffer time will be allocated as required during each stage of the Process Model to forestall the human tendency to use buffer time, whether it is needed or not.
- *Use no-blame reviews* - Each milestone and post-milestone review should be conducted in an atmosphere that is construc-

tive, rather than destructive. Examine what could have been performed more efficiently and work to achieve it, rather than trying to assign blame, which can be harmful to the team dynamic.

MSF, MOF, and the Project Management Discipline

It is important to understand that the MSF Process Model is not completely autonomous, but intersects with MOF and the Project Management Discipline in a number of areas. The Release Management team role should include representatives from operations, thereby ensuring the presence of IT staff familiar with MOF throughout the entire project. During the Stabilizing and Deploying Phases, MSF and MOF combine to meet common deployment and operations objectives. The solution and all accompanying documentation are handed over to IT operations, and responsibility is shifted from the project team as they disengage from the project.

It must also be understood that many of the underlying principles of the MSF Process Model have their roots in the MSF Team Model. This distinguishes MSF from traditional forms of project management. These principles encourage the sharing of duties among different role clusters according to the current phase of the Process Model.

4. Process Model - Envisioning Phase

Overview

The mission of the Envisioning Phase is the assembly of the core team and production of a unified vision/scope document. It is crucial for the team, customer, and other key stakeholders to agree on the vision and scope for the solution and be able to state this clearly and unambiguously. The vision statement can be used by everyone involved in the project to remind them of what they are attempting to achieve and keep them motivated toward their individual and project goals. It is also important during this phase to have a high-level view of the tasks needed to carry out the project; the MSF Risk Management Discipline can be used to identify initial risks that may become a threat to success.

During this phase, the project team is assembled into the appropriate role clusters and MSF Readiness Management practices are applied to ensure that all needed competencies are present. If the required skill levels have not yet been met, knowledge gaps should be identified and appropriate training plans organized to ensure these do not pose significant risk. It is also possible to pair team members with more experienced individuals to enhance existing skills while training is organized or merely to boost the overall experience level of the role cluster. It should be noted that although the team is assembled during this phase, not all team members may necessarily be present, since they might not be required at this time.

Additionally, there must be a careful business-needs analysis to determine which problems the solution must address. Any early constraints to the project need to be identified and trade-offs made. At this point, a high-level view of the solution is developed, with the majority of the work occurring during the Planning Phase. In this phase, MSF can cross into MOF through the common Release

Manager role in both frameworks. Further, a close relationship between the MSF Product Management role cluster and the MOF Service role cluster during this phase will ensure that needed features from an operations and service management perspective are added to the vision/scope document from the beginning of the project.

Figure 4.1 shows the interim and major milestones associated with the Envisioning Phase.

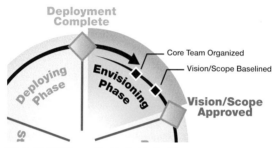

Figure 4.1 MSF Process Model - Envisioning Phase

Key Elements
Role Clusters
The primary role within the Envisioning Phase is Product Management, due to the close involvement of the customer and the other key stakeholders. It is imperative that all parties have a unified understanding of what the project is trying to achieve. Product Management acts as an intermediary between team and customer. Table 4.1 shows the roles and their corresponding focus within the Envisioning Phase.

Role	Focus
Product Management	Overall goals, business-needs analysis, vision/scope document
Program Management	Project structure document, solution concept, design goals
Development	Feasibility study, technology research and analysis
Test	Testing strategies and acceptance criteria
Release Management	Deployment implications, operations management, operational acceptance criteria
User Experience	User expectations

Table 4.1 Envisioning Phase: Focus by Role

Deliverables

In the Envisioning Phase, the team produces the following deliverables:

- *Vision/Scope Document* - This document contains a statement of the vision for the project and the intended scope of the project toward fulfilling that vision. Vision can be defined as an unbounded view of the solution, which can also be seen as an ultimate statement of goals. The statement should be succinct and should be used by the team to ensure they are heading in the right direction at all times. Whenever the team is unsure of project progress, the vision can motivate, reinforce, and maintain focus. The document also needs to contain a problem statement, which identifies the current issues facing the business that need to be addressed and helps to identify the scope and validity of the project. The scope of the solution defines the aspect of the vision that can be fulfilled within the bounds of the project and can be broken down into two distinct aspects:

  - <u>Solution scope</u> - The actual products and services that will be produced by the solution in this current release.
  - <u>Project scope</u> - The work to be performed by the team to produce the solution as set down by the solution scope.

At this stage, the solution scope identifies the aspects of the solution that are critical to success. This can be seen as a 'version 1.0' solution in which critical functionality must be delivered, while extra functionality can be left to future iterations of the solution. This should not imply, however, that the scope is frozen at this point. It is expected that the scope will experience a certain amount of change during the project life cycle. This exercise also helps to set customer and other key stakeholder expectations for the solution and helps to ensure converged goals between customer, other key stakeholders, and team.

- *Risk Assessment Document* - An initial identification of risks to the project, following the procedures identified in the MSF Risk Management Discipline. Each risk will be outlined along with a description of impact to the project if the risk should occur, the chance of the risk occurring, and possible mitigation plans to reduce the possibility of risk occurrence.
- *Project Structure Document* - Serves as a logistical and organizational document for the project. Maps out information on team members, customers and other key stakeholders and how to contact them. It also covers standard project administration information such as mailing list addresses, shared locations for project documents, and recurring meetings.

Interim Milestones

There are two Interim Milestones in the Envisioning Phase:

- *Core Team Organized* - At this point, the major team members have been identified and assigned to appropriate role clusters. The project structure document has been created and disseminated to all involved parties.
- *Vision/Scope Baselined* - This Interim Milestone is reached when the draft of the vision/scope document is delivered to all involved parties for review. During this time, comments and suggestions can be made and the document can be refined to the point where it is acceptable to everyone before progressing to the major milestone.

Major Milestone - Vision/Scope Approved

At this point, the team, customers, and other key stakeholders have agreed on the vision and scope of the solution. They are prepared to move forward into the Planning Phase. At the *Vision/Scope Approved Milestone*, there has been agreement on what will be delivered initially with the solution. Basic time factors will have been decided upon, although the majority of scheduling work will be done during the Planning Phase.

Milestone Review and Approval

The Envisioning Milestone review meeting can be used as an opportunity for the team, customer and other key stakeholders, to air any concerns regarding trade-offs, risks, and readiness issues that may need to be resolved, along with a timeline for resolution. At this meeting, the deliverables will be presented and final approval to continue the project will be received. At this point, the vision/scope of the project has been baselined but not frozen. Change control processes will be implemented from this point onwards, which will address any change to the scope.

MSF, a pocket guide

5. Process Model - Planning Phase

Overview

The overall goal of this phase is to answer three extremely important questions:

- *What* are we going to build?
- *How* are we going to build it?
- *When* are we going to build it?

The answers to these questions, in the form of the phase deliverables, will allow the team to move forward into the next phase and actually begin building the solution. The tasks that must be performed and the schedules for performing them will have been determined. At the end of the Planning Phase, a development/test environment will have been set up.

The project vision and scope remain extremely important during this phase, since it is imperative that the plan maintain traceability to the project vision and scope. Traceability ensures that any planning pertaining to the features of the project can be directly traced back to some aspect of the vision or scope of the project, as captured during the Envisioning Phase. This is not to say that features outside the scope can never be included. The project development is considered an iterative and dynamic activity. There will, however, need to be review and agreement between the team and the customer before any alteration to the scope of the project can be approved. The previously mentioned trade-off triangle can be used to assess the feasibility of any such alteration to ensure that there is no negative impact on the existing vision/scope and plan in terms of the schedule, resources, and features.

The concept of planning in MSF is vital, as it greatly reduces risks that can lead to missed deadlines, budget overruns, and the product defects that a lack of planning can produce. It is important to stress, however, that excessive planning can result in a team that is paralyzed by its desire to plan and analyze. This phase concludes with the team and customers having a clear idea of what will be delivered and when the team will deliver it.

During this phase, MSF overlaps with MOF when the Request for Change (RFC) document is created. The RFC will be passed to the appropriate change management committees as part of the MOF Changing Quadrant. Attention should also be paid to the personnel involved in the MOF Optimizing and Supporting Quadrants, who may have additional requirements for the project. Their input (such as testing and support plans) may be a response to the need to comply with service level agreements (SLAs), to perform service-desk tasks, to provide Availability Management, or other service management functions (SMFs). Members of MSF's Release Management role can play a leading part in this process. Members of the User Experience role will also be involved as part of the Readiness Management Discipline, as training plans are developed.

Figure 5.1 shows the interim and major milestones associated with the Planning Phase.

Figure 5.1 MSF Process Model - Planning Phase

Key Elements

Role Clusters

This phase is driven by the Program Management role, due to the fundamental activities of scheduling, design, and logistics that permeate it. Program Management is highly concerned with all of these activities, and keeping the project on track in terms of work and schedule. Other role clusters have different focuses, which can be seen in table 5.1.

Role	Focus
Product Management	Business-needs Analysis, Solution Conceptual Design, Communications Plan
Program Management	Functional Specification, Solution Conceptual and Logical Design, Budgets, Master Project Plan and Schedule
Development	Technology Validation, Logical and Physical Design, Development Plan/Schedule
Test	Requirements, Test Plan, Test Schedule, Evaluation of Solution Design in Conjunction with Release Management
Release Management	Operations Issues and Requirements, Evaluation of Solution Design, Pilot/Deployment Plan and Schedule
User Experience	Training and Documentation Plan/Schedule, User Needs, Usage Scenarios, Accessibility and Localization Issues

Table 5.1 Planning Phase: Focus by Role

Deliverables

In the Planning Phase, the team produces the following deliverables:

- *Functional Specification* - This document is the result of the conceptual, logical, and physical design process and maps out how the different features of the solution will appear and function in the target environment. This specification is extremely important for a number of reasons:
  - It forces the team and customer to agree on exactly what they are building.
  - Developers can use the functional specification to ensure their

development activities are on track and correct.
- It allows the team to make reasonable estimates on schedule, cost, and skill sets needed for development of the project.

> The **functional specification** develops from the following design processes:
> • *Conceptual Design* - Examines business and user needs in detail to provide a reasonable picture of what is needed from the solution, through the processes of user profiling and storyboarding.
> • *Logical Design* - Details the 'building blocks' of the solution and how they interrelate with each other. This design does not provide technical implementation details.
> • *Physical Design* - Provides information, through a technical design of the solution, on the components, technologies and services that will be used to develop the solution.

Figure 5.2 MSF Design Processes

• *Risk Management Plan* - This plan details what will be done to ensure risks do not endanger the project as described in the MSF Risk Management Discipline. It is a logical progression of the risk management document produced during the Envisioning Phase.
• *Master Project Plan* - The plan is a collection of the planning documents compiled by each of the role clusters, with a focus on their particular concerns. They combine to describe how the solution will be created. There are no strict rules as to which plans must be developed; however, table 5.2 provides some guidance.

Plan	Responsible Role
Customer Communication Plan	Product Management
Solution Testing Plan	Test
Budget and Purchasing Plan	Program Management
Solution Development Plan	Development
Pilot Deployment Plan	Release Management
User and Operations Training Plan	User Experience
Production Deployment Plan	Release Management
Security Plan	Development/Release Management

Table 5.2 Roles and Project Plans

- *Master Project Schedule* - The collection of scheduling documents, as compiled by the role clusters, representing a timeline for the project. Each role will produce a schedule that is submitted to Program Management for integration into the master project schedule.

Interim Milestones

The following Interim Milestones are associated with the Planning Phase:

- *Technology Validation Complete* - At this stage, the intended technologies to be used for the solution have been examined to ensure that they will perform as specified in a production-modeled environment. It is important to understand that at this point, the team has merely proven that the technologies will work in an ideal environment. Actual proof-of-concept for the customer's production environment will occur during the next phase.
- *Functional Specification Baselined* - This Interim Milestone is reached with the draft of the functional specification document being delivered to all involved parties for review. During this time, comments and suggestions can be made and the document can be refined to the point where it is acceptable to all parties before progressing to the major milestone.
- *Master Project Plan Baselined* - All individual plans are submitted

by the role clusters and assembled into a draft of the master project plan for dissemination to the team and customer for review and discussion.

- *Master Project Schedule Baselined* - Similar to the master project plan, all role clusters submit their individual schedules to Program Management for compilation into the master project schedule. Program Management may make changes in consultation with role clusters and the customer to ensure release dates are met.
- *Development and Test Environment Set Up* - This milestone is achieved when a development and test environment has been established that is separate from production, but mirrors it as closely as possible. Equipment will have been purchased and allocated. Appropriate images will have been created to return development and test equipment to baseline standard configurations as quickly as possible, so that another cycle of development and testing can begin.

Major Milestone - Project Plans Approved

At this milestone, the functional specification, plans, and schedule for the project are approved by the team, the customer, and the other key stakeholders and it is now acceptable to move to the Developing Phase.

Milestone Review and Approval

During the milestone review meeting, the sponsor, customer, and other key stakeholders give their formal approval of the functional specification, plans, and schedule. From this point, these documents are considered approved and placed under change control, so proper authorization can be used to combat the possibility of scope creep during the rest of the project. Trade-offs may occur during this meeting as the resources, schedule and features of the project are reviewed. Moreover, investigation of team skill sets will be checked to ensure readiness management processes are being followed.

As the final act of the Planning Phase, the RFC will be submitted to IT operations as part of the MOF Changing Quadrant. At this point, the master project plan is considered approved and the vision/scope document can be revised, or rewritten, to bring it in line with any changes in scope that may have been agreed upon during this phase.

Overview

During the Developing Phase, all aspects of the solution are built, tested, and traced back to the functional specification to ensure they comply with previous agreements. There is a commonly held misconception that the Developing Phase is primarily concerned with writing code. It is important to note that this phase also develops all other aspects of the solution such as support infra-structure, documentation, user training courses, operations guides, and many other deliverables. Project Management practices of task, time, and cost management are important during this phase. The use of feature or function teams on larger projects will mean that some role clusters are assigned to multiple teams. This phase also overlaps with MOF as Release Management coordinates with the Operations and Support role clusters during the development of operations plans, and both operations and support documentation.

Figure 6.1 shows the interim and major milestones associated with the Developing Phase.

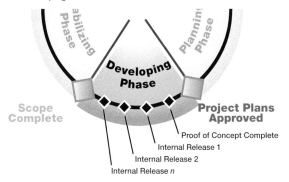

Figure 6.1 MSF Process Model - Developing Phase

Key Elements

Role Clusters

The driving role behind this phase is Development, although Test, Release Management and User Experience are also key roles. Development drives the building of the solution's major aspects and the infrastructure to support it within the organization. Because of this, the Development and Test roles are shielded from contact with the customer or other key stakeholders. The idea behind this is that the Development and Test roles should not be exposed to situations that may distract from the prevailing needs of building and testing the solution. The role clusters active in this phase and their focus are seen in table 6.1.

Role	Focus
Product Management	Customer Communication, Manage Expectations
Program Management	Schedule Tracking, Functional Specification Tracking, Plan Tracking
Development	Code/Infrastructure
User Experience	Training Development, User Interface, Usability Testing
Test	Test Plans, Bug Triaging, Documentation Testing
Release Management	Rollout Plans, Pilot Plans, Operations Documentation, Site Logistics

Table 6.1 Developing Phase: Focus by Role

Deliverables

In the Developing Phase, the team produces the following deliverables:

- *Source Code and Binaries* - Uncompiled source code for the solution and compiled binary executables.
- *Installation Scripts* - Unattended setup files that are used to set up the lab environment. This can be useful if the customer needs to replicate the environment in future projects.
- *Configuration Settings* - Details on all configurations performed on the development servers to aid in environment replication at a later stage.

- *Frozen Functional Specification* - At the Scope Complete Milestone, the functional specification should be frozen to prevent further development on new features during the Stabilizing Phase.
- *Performance Support Elements* - Baselining utilities and benchmarking tools used during the Developing Phase.
- *Test Specifications and Test Cases* - These can be beneficial after the solution is deployed to ensure compliance to expected performance levels and test cases can be used when recommending the solution to other clients.

Deliverables also include documentation, training, marketing material, and infrastructural elements such as images for servers, and so forth. It is possible that changes were made to the master plans and schedules during this phase; in this case the revised documents must also be delivered.

Interim Milestones

The following Interim Milestones are associated with the Developing Phase:

- *Proof of Concept Complete* - This involves proving the solution's infrastructure will function as specified in a simulation of the production environment. This is distinct from the activities of technology validation carried out during the Planning Phase, which tests from the perspective of a nonproduction, pristine environment. This is important because if the infrastructure does not function in this environment, it is highly likely that the finished solution will suffer from the same problem. Once this is complete, all custom aspects of the solution can be built and the interim testing and release cycles can begin.
- *Interim Release 1, 2, and so on* - These milestones are representative of internal releases of the solution, which are tested for bugs and validated through tracing back to the functional specification. This can be done through the concept of the 'daily build'

which is a regular compilation and test of the solution components. This process is considered a best practice and is used within Microsoft for many of their projects. It allows constant review and traceability testing to ensure the solution is meeting all requirements. One of the benefits of the internal release cycle is that it allows different features of the solution to be developed as part of an internal release and helps to break down tasks and show progress toward the completed solution to the team.

Major Milestone - Scope Complete

At this point, all aspects of the solution have been developed and tested internally for bugs and stability issues. The solution is now ready to be tested and stabilized outside of the development environment.

Milestone Review and Approval

At this stage, the team and customer meet to review the deliverables and evaluate their adherence to the functional specification. After approval is gained, the team is ready to proceed to the Stabilizing Phase. Again, the trade-off triangle, Readiness Management plans, and Risk Assessment document will be used to ensure the team is on track. The scope is frozen at this point to ensure that no development work begins on new features during the Stabilizing Phase.

7. Process Model - Stabilizing Phase

Overview

In the Stabilizing Phase the team moves from the duties of building the solution to ensuring the solution is as free of bugs and issues as possible in preparation for final deployment. At this time, the solution is tested in a pilot environment, bugs are tracked and resolved, and user acceptance testing is completed. Code is not the only aspect of the solution to be tested, since user training, documentation and operations procedures are also examined prior to the Release Readiness Approved Milestone. At this point the solution is considered complete, has been accepted as meeting the requirements as in the vision/scope document, and is stable enough to deploy into production and to hand over to operations.

Figure 7.1 shows the interim and major milestones associated with the Stabilizing Phase.

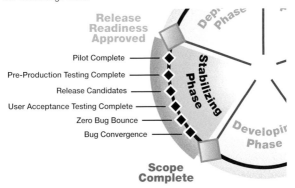

Figure 7.1 MSF Process Model - Stabilizing Phase

Key Elements

Role Clusters

This phase is primarily driven by the Release Management and Test roles, due to the close relationship with operations and a need for the solution to be stable and bug free. Other role clusters have duties during this phase as noted in table 7.1.

Role	Focus
Product Management	Product Launch Plans, Customer Relations
Program Management	Schedule, Bug Tracking
Development	Solution Optimization, Bug Resolution
User Experience	Refinement of Training Materials and Acceptance Testing
Test	Testing, Bug Reports
Release Management	Deployment Plan, Operations and Support Training, Pilot Testing

Table 7.1 Stabilizing Phase: Focus by Role

Deliverables

In the Stabilizing Phase, the team produces the following deliverables:

- *Gold Release* - These are release-ready versions of the following components:
  - Source Code and Binaries.
  - Release Notes.
  - Documentation, Help and Training Materials.
  - Operations Support Documentation and Installation Scripts.
- *Test Results and Bug Deficiency Reports* - These can be used by operations when conducting a performance baseline of the infrastructure and when determining any possible bug deficiencies that might be active during the production rollout.
- *Project Documentation* - By-products of the project that are not directly related to the product but that will be used for reference during Deployment.

Interim Milestones

The following Interim Milestones are associated with the Stabilizing Phase:

- *Bug Convergence* - This milestone represents a moment in time where the rate at which bugs are resolved exceeds the rate at which bugs are found. This will not manifest itself suddenly, but is likely to be a gradual trend, and represents the progress made in terms of bug resolution. Once at this point, the number of outstanding bugs should continue to decrease.

- *Zero Bug Bounce* - This represents a point where there are no active bugs. It should not be assumed that no other bugs will be discovered, but it does show a marked improvement and positive step toward the final code, known as the gold release.

- *User Acceptance Testing Complete* - At this time, users have finished testing the solution in a nonproduction environment to ensure that all business and customer needs are being met. Operational support personnel are trained on support procedures. Special attention is also given to possible critical issues that may prevent the solution from being released.

- *Release Candidates* - These are a number of feature-complete releases deployed to the test environment as possible candidates for release to the live pilot environment. Any issues are reported and resolved and new release candidates are deployed before the solution is considered ready for pilot.

- *Pre-Production Testing Complete* - This ensures that all aspects of the solution are ready for the pilot environment. All support issues should have been resolved; the pilot site and all documentation should be prepared and complete.

- *Pilot Complete* - During the pilot, the solution is tested in a live production environment with a subset of the user population. Data is gathered to determine suitability for full deployment and once complete, the team decides whether to move to the major milestone and Deploying Phase. In contrast, it may be decided to roll back to a previous state, as a result of issues uncovered during the pilot.

Major Milestone - Release Readiness Approved

At this milestone, the team transfers management and support responsibility to IT operations and prepares to conduct the deployment.

Milestone Review and Approval

During the milestone review, source code as well as hardware specifications will be placed into the MOF Definitive Software Library (DSL) and all documentation and support information will be transferred to operations. The team now begins plans to deploy the solution in the production environment.

Overview

At the end of the Stabilizing Phase, the operations and support staff approve the solution. This phase represents a critical overlapping point between MSF and MOF. During the Deploying Phase, the solution is deployed in the production environment and the team disengages from the project over time, progressively handing over all responsibility to IT operations. The culmination of the Deploying Phase results in the final sign-off by the customer. It also is where the team gets together to do a post-mortem of the project to examine what went well, what went badly, and what could have been done better. Their conclusions are documented for use in future projects.

Figure 8.1 shows the interim and major milestones associated with the Deploying Phase.

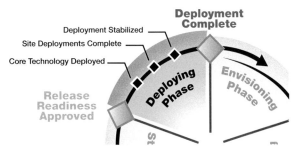

Figure 8.1 MSF Process Model - Deploying Phase

Key Elements

Role Clusters

Table 8.1 shows team roles and focus during the Deploying Phase.

Role	Focus
Product Management	Customer Sign-Off, Feedback and Project Assessment
Program Management	Stabilization, Comparison of Solution and Scope
Development	Problem Resolution, Escalation
User Experience	Training
Test	Performance/Training Testing
Release Management	Deployment Management, Change Approval

Table 8.1 Deploying Phase: Focus by Role

Deliverables

In the Deploying Phase, the team produces the following deliverables:

- *Support and Operations Information Systems* - Data, procedures and other materials created during the project that will enhance the support of the product in production.
- *Document Repository* - Including all code, documentation, and load tests.
- *Project Closeout Report* - Including project financials, customer surveys and lessons learned.

Interim Milestones

The following Interim Milestones are associated with the Deploying Phase:

- *Core Technology Deployed* - At this milestone, the core components to support the solution have been deployed and certified as stable. Core components include the necessary infrastructure support elements such as switches, routers, domain controllers, firewalls, and so on.

- *Site Deployments Complete* - Site deployment involves ensuring the solution is functional and stable at each site and all users have access to it. Each site deployment involves a four-stage, 'mini project' which involves preparing and installing the site deployment, conducting user and support-staff training, and stabilizing the solution before signing off and retiring from the site.
- *Deployment Stabilized* - At this point, the customer and team come to an agreement that the solution is stable and operating at expected levels. The team begins to disengage from the project and formally transfer responsibility to operations. When the deployment is stable, but before the Deployment Complete Milestone, the project goes through the 'Quiet Period'. This is a period of time where the team monitors and baselines the solution and deals with any support issues that may arise.

Major Milestone - Deployment Complete

At the Deployment Complete Milestone, sign-offs have been completed, and the team formally disengages from the project. At this point, a closeout report is created and provided to the customer. This report is a collection of all documentation and user satisfaction data generated by a user satisfaction survey. The sign-off indicates that the customer is satisfied with the solution and signals the formal end of the project.

Milestone Review and Approval

After obtaining sign-off, a post-mortem review is performed between members of the project team to determine what could have been done better and what was considered successful. If the team is intending to begin a new iteration of the project, this review can be used to provide suggestions for areas identified as needing improvement, and how those improvements could be achieved.

9. MSF Disciplines

Overview

MSF defines three disciplines, or areas of practice, that functionally align with the core principles and key concepts of the MSF Team and Process Models. This set of disciplines enables optimal application of the MSF Team and Process Models within a diverse range of contemporary business environments. Based on well-known bodies of knowledge, each MSF discipline provides prescriptive guidance consisting of approaches, methods, and techniques for use in a specific area.

Risk Management Discipline

The MSF Risk Management Discipline describes a proactive approach for effectively managing the inherent uncertainties associated with technology projects. By incorporating risk management into activities and deliverables of the project as well as distributing the responsibility of managing project risk to each team role, the MSF Risk Management Discipline establishes a proactive and holistic approach to managing risk that increases the probability of successfully accomplishing project objectives. Central to the MSF Risk Management Discipline is a six-step risk management process that is visible, measurable, and repeatable.

Readiness Management Discipline

The MSF Readiness Management Discipline describes an approach for measuring the *readiness* state of individuals within an organization. Readiness is defined as the degree to which the current state of individual knowledge, skills, and abilities matches that of the desired state. The Readiness Management Discipline provides guidance for defining, assessing, changing, and evaluating the knowledge, skills, and abilities of project teams.

Project Management Discipline

Whereas traditional project management is performed in an environment characterized by hierarchical organization and management structures, the MSF Project Management Discipline provides a distributed approach to project management whereby specific project management activities, such as planning and scheduling, are shared among the various roles and team members.

Integration with Models

Each of the MSF Disciplines is well integrated with the MSF Team and Process Models. This integration provides flexible and effective guidance for ensuring successful project delivery. While integration of the MSF Project Management Discipline occurs primarily through distribution of project management responsibilities, the MSF Risk Management Discipline provides integration using definitions of specific role responsibilities as well as project life cycle activities and milestone deliverables. Integration of the MSF Readiness Management Discipline occurs through an understanding and assessment of the roles, functional areas, and responsibilities of each member of the project team.

10. Risk Management Discipline

Overview

The contemporary IT project life cycle is highly dynamic. It is characterized by compressed schedules, frequent change, and high levels of uncertainty. Effectively managing this uncertainty is a critical success factor for delivering today's technology solution projects. MSF provides a core discipline for managing project uncertainty known as the MSF Risk Management Discipline. This discipline advocates an approach to managing project risk whereby potential problems are identified, assessed, and managed by the project team on a continuous and proactive basis. The MSF Risk Management Discipline is well integrated with the MSF Team and Process Models. This enables it to serve as a useful tool for guiding critical decision-making activities as well as facilitating the creation of project plans and schedules.

- *Proactive Approach* - MSF's approach to risk management is proactive and based on a process that involves continuously assessing what can go wrong with a project and deciding how to respond. Proactive risk management allows the team to:
  - Anticipate potential problems.
  - Focus on root causes of a problem rather than the symptoms.
  - Prevent and minimize risk through mitigation rather than just reacting to consequences.
  - Prepare for risk consequences in advance.
  - Use a known, structured, visible process versus an ad hoc approach.
- *A Six-Step Process* - The MSF Risk Management Discipline consists of a six-step, logically ordered process that facilitates the identification of priorities and enables the project team to make project decisions based on perceived threats and opportunities. The output of this process is a Risk Assessment document, which serves as a 'living' record of the high-priority risks associ-

ated with the project. It is used throughout the project life cycle to prioritize effort, drive decisions, highlight dependencies, determine schedules, and educate management.

Characteristics of Risk

MSF broadly describes project risk as any condition or event that may have a positive or negative effect on the outcome of a project. This wider concept of *speculative risk* is utilized by the financial industry, where decisions regarding uncertainties may be associated with the potential for gain as well as losses. Speculative risk differs from the concept of *pure risk* used by the insurance industry, where the uncertainties are associated with potential losses only. The nature of loss within a project can be financial as well as related to project schedule and product quality. It is important to note that risk is not synonymous with a problem or issue. Whereas risk refers to a future *possibility* of loss or other aberrant outcome, a problem refers to a present condition affecting a project. If not effectively managed, a risk may evolve into an issue or problem. Moreover, project risk should be viewed as neither intrinsically good nor bad, but rather as an element to be managed. While an unmanaged risk may result in a negative outcome, a potential problem identified and managed in advance improves the probability of success.

Principles of Successful Risk Management

Successfully managing project risk requires an understanding of several key principles and concepts:

- *Risk management is an on-going process* - It is important to recognize that the most effective approach to managing project risk is one in which uncertainties are identified, analyzed, and addressed in a proactive and continuous manner.
- *Risk management is a shared responsibility* - The management of project risk is not just the responsibility of one person or role, but rather it is a responsibility of the entire project team. While the

project manager is responsible for driving the overall risk management process, effective risk management often involves the assignment of risk-related action items to team members.

- *Risk management should be viewed in a positive light* - A 'blame-free' environment must be established allowing team members to openly identify and discuss potential risks without fear of reprisal, retribution, or ridicule.
- *Risk management must be integrated into the project management activity* - Action plans resulting from the risk management process must be incorporated into the master project plan and master project schedule. In general, high-risk, high-need items should be addressed first in order to provide sufficient time for mitigation.
- *Successful risk management requires specificity and clarity* - Risk statements and action plans must be clear and unambiguous. Language that is broad and generic in nature will increase uncertainty in members of the project team. This may result in different interpretations of risk items, priorities, and plans, which is a risk in itself.

The Risk Management Process

The MSF Risk Management Discipline embodies a six-step process for managing project uncertainties. This process facilitates a proactive approach to risk management by logically defining a set of activities that support the transformation of broadly focused risk events into quantified threats, along with plans and actions. Depicted in figure 10.1, the six steps of the MSF risk management process are: *Identify, Analyze and Prioritize, Plan and Schedule, Track and Report, Control,* and *Learn*. The output of this process is a risk assessment document as well as a risk knowledge base. The risk assessment document incorporates the high-priority project risks and is used to guide decision making as well as project planning. The risk knowledge base serves as a repository of 'lessons learned' that can be used to facilitate risk management of future projects.

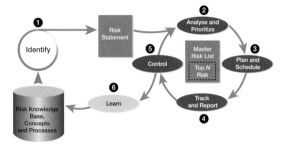

Figure 10.1 MSF Risk Management Process Diagram

Step 1: Risk Identification

The initial step of the MSF risk management process is to identify the risks or uncertainties facing the project. Involving all members of the project team as well as key stakeholders, the risk identification activity seeks to discover potential problems that may derail successful delivery of the project. To facilitate risk identification, MSF recommends the use of risk classifications, which are ready-made lists of project areas that should be examined. Using risk classifications enables the project team to consider the broad spectrum of factors that may affect the outcome of the project.

Risk Statements

The primary output of the risk identification step is an initial list of risk statements. A risk statement consists of two distinct elements: a risk condition and a risk consequence. While a risk condition describes a condition, event, or state that the project team believes may adversely (or aberrantly) affect the project, a risk consequence describes the ensuing loss that may be realized should the risk condition become a reality.

Step 2: Risk Analysis and Prioritization

The primary goal of the risk analysis and prioritization step is to establish a priority for risk events, so that project resources can be committed to those risks that pose the greatest threat to the project.

Risk Probability

Risk analysis begins by estimating the probability of occurrence for a risk event. Rather than using a qualitative assessment, MSF recommends the use of a simple, numerical scale for assignment of probability values. In order to facilitate risk comparison and assessment, it is important that the selected scale be used consistently throughout the life cycle of the project.

Risk Impact

The next task is to assess the impact of the risk to the project. Risk impact represents a measure of loss or other adverse effect to the project resulting from the occurrence of the risk. As with risk probability, the use of a numerical scale to assess risk impact is recommended. The scale used for risk impact should be agreed upon by the project team and used consistently throughout the project life cycle.

Risk Exposure

The next task involves determining the exposure or quantified threat of each risk. The MSF Risk Management Discipline provides a simple method for determining the threat of a risk event in which risk probability is multiplied by risk impact.

Prioritized Master Risk List

The final task is to create a prioritized master risk list. Risk priorities are established by sorting risk entries on the basis of risk exposure. The master risk list is a 'living document' that is used to facilitate tracking and management of high-exposure risks. Once the master risk list is sorted by risk exposure, the set of risk events that pose the greatest threat to the success of the project, referred to as the 'top *n* risks', become the focus of the project team. The master risk list typically addresses the following aspects of risk:

- Priority.
- Condition.
- Consequence.
- Probability.
- Impact.
- Exposure.
- Mitigation.
- Contingency.
- Triggers.
- Owners.
- Status.

Step 3: Risk Planning and Scheduling

The goal of the risk planning and scheduling step is to develop a risk management plan that addresses those risks that pose the greatest threat to the project. The risk management plan describes the strategies, approaches, and techniques that will be employed to prevent or minimize risk occurrence as well as impact.

Risk Mitigation

The essence of risk mitigation planning is the identification of actions and activities that will be performed in advance to either eliminate the risk, or otherwise to reduce the probability of occurrence and impact to a level that is acceptable for the project. It is important to note that risk mitigation is not synonymous with risk avoidance. Whereas risk avoidance is a strategy in which project scope is modified in order to eliminate high-risk events, risk mitigation is focused on risk minimization. There may be cases, however, in which project risk cannot be effectively mitigated. In these situations, MSF recommends that an emphasis be placed on the development of contingency plans in order to minimize risk consequences.

Risk Contingencies

Risk contingencies describe an organized and pre-planned response to a risk event that occurs despite 'best-effort' mitigation activities. Executed in response to triggering events, risk contingency plans are developed by the project team well in advance, and address what actions will be performed in order to minimize risk impact.

Contingency Plan Triggers

Triggers are a key element in risk contingency planning as they signal when to execute a risk contingency plan. MSF defines three types of triggers: point-in-time, threshold, and event-based. Whereas point-in-time triggers are based on calendar dates, threshold triggers are based on entities that can be counted or measured. Event-based triggers rely on the occurrence of specific events or activities.

Step 4: Risk Tracking and Reporting

The primary goal of the risk tracking and reporting step is to monitor the status of implemented risk action plans as well as provide notification of triggering events.

Risk Tracking

Risk tracking serves as the 'watchdog' function of a risk action plan, and provides assurance that mitigation and contingency plans are being executed in a timely manner. While the majority of effort expended by the project team is focused on carrying out risk mitigation plans, other types of risk action plans such as research and risk transference are also addressed during this step.

Risk Reporting

Risk reporting is concerned with communicating risk status to the project team as well as to the stakeholders. At the team level, risk reporting occurs on a regular basis where the status of each risk event, including execution status of mitigation and contingency plans, is reported and analyzed. Risk reporting at the stakeholder level typically involves presenting status of the highest exposure project risks along with a summary of associated risk management plans.

Step 5: Risk Control

The risk control step effectively implements changes as identified during the risk tracking and reporting step. Among other activities, risk mitigation plans are implemented during this step in conjunction with contingency plans in response to trigger notifications. Moreover, risks that have been successfully mitigated or otherwise dealt with are retired as part of this step.

Step 6: Risk Learning

The final step of the MSF risk management process is learning. The primary goals of this step are to capture and formalize knowledge acquired during the risk management process as well as provide quality assurance on risk management activities. Also referred to as 'risk leverage', risk learning provides a strategic benefit to the enterprise through enhanced project team capabilities as well as an improved risk management process.

Risk Knowledge Base

Risk learning is a continuous activity and is primarily focused on capturing lessons-learned associated with risk identification and mitigation activities. These lessons-learned contribute to the enterprise risk knowledge base, which is a highly accessible repository of artifacts including risk classifications and risk mitigation plans.

Risk Management Process Improvement

A secondary focus of risk learning is improving the risk management process. Regular risk review meetings, involving all members of the project team, provide a forum for discussing project risks as well as capturing feedback on the risk management process.

11. Readiness Management Discipline

Overview

The MSF Readiness Management Discipline provides a proactive approach for effectively managing the knowledge, skills, and abilities of project teams engaged in the planning, building, and deployment of technology solutions. This discipline describes a collection of fundamental principles as well as proven plans and practices for following a readiness management process.

Characteristics of Readiness

As illustrated in figure 11.1, MSF characterizes readiness as the degree to which the current state of knowledge, skills, and abilities matches that of the desired future state. The MSF Readiness Management Discipline provides guidance and processes for assessing and acquiring the knowledge, skills, and abilities to enable effective solution development as well as Enterprise Architecture (EA) planning.

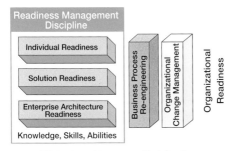

Figure 11.1 MSF Readiness Management Discipline Components

Applying Readiness Management

The MSF Readiness Management Discipline is well integrated with the MSF Team and Process Models. Each role on a project team includes key functional areas that individuals performing in those roles must be capable of fulfilling. Individual readiness is the measurement of the state of an individual with regard to the knowledge, skills and abilities needed to meet the responsibilities required of their particular role. At the organizational level, readiness refers to the current state of the collective measurements of readiness. Learning plans are created for any proficiency gaps identified during the assessment. These plans help ensure that required proficiencies are available to the project when needed.

Envisioning Phase

During the Envisioning Phase, a key deliverable known as the project structure document is created. Among other things, this document captures the organizational and administrative structure for a project. In terms of Readiness Management, the project structure document can be used to record the approach the project team will take in preparing itself for the project. Readiness information that is captured in the project structure document includes identification of individuals assigned to perform proficiency assessments as well as mechanisms for determining project scenarios and associated proficiency levels.

Planning Phase

Detailed project plans, task assignments, and schedules are created during the Planning Phase. Moreover, it is during this phase that team level proficiency assessments are performed. The results of these assessments are subsequently used to develop and implement plans for addressing identified skill gaps.

Developing Phase

With skill gaps addressed, the project team is able to effectively carry out the activities of building and testing the product. During the latter stages of the Developing Phase, the product is typically made available to the enterprise, on an incremental basis, for review and evaluation. From an organizational readiness perspective, this is an ideal time for the project team to assess the value of activities related to readying product owners and end users for their involvement during this phase.

Stabilizing and Deploying Phases

During these final two stages of the project life cycle, most of the readiness activities have either been completed or are nearing completion. A major readiness activity that is performed during the Deploying Phase is training, which involves preparing users as well as support and operations personnel for the release of the product.

Skills Required for the MSF Team Roles

A key attribute of the MSF Team Model is the definition of six project roles and their alignment to six project performance goals, as described in table 2.1. The MSF Readiness Management Discipline can be used to proactively correlate unique skill set requirements for a given project to a project role. Table 11.1 highlights skills and responsibilities for each role as defined by the MSF Team Model.

Product Management
Proven experience managing the product life cycle
Ability to research and synthesize business wants and needs into solution requirements
Ability to prioritize requirements and features for each versioned release
Ability to generate or stimulate solution demand via marketing programs and activities

Program Management
Proven experience in managing projects and teams
Experience and skills in facilitation, negotiation, and communications
Ability to drive and manage critical trade-off decisions
Proven project administration experience and skills

Development
Proven experience in leading a solution development team
Technical expertise in solution-related products and technologies
Understanding of principles and practices related to the development of application and infrastructure components

Test
Proven experience and skills in test planning, test engineering, and test reporting
Understanding of principles and practices related to the development of application and infrastructure components
Understanding of various testing standards, tools, processes, and procedures

Release Management
Proven experience in releasing and deploying a solution to a production environment
Ability to lead and manage a release management team
Technical expertise in solution-related hardware and software components

User Experience
Proven experience in developing user-performance support materials for a solution
Ability to derive end-user requirements and translate requirements into the solution design
Good understanding of usability principles and concepts

Table 11.1 Skills and Responsibilities

Principles of Successful Readiness Management

An understanding of the key principles, concepts, and practices of the MSF approach to Readiness Management is required in order to successfully manage readiness at any level.

Readiness Principles

The following principles are associated with the Readiness Management Discipline:

- *Foster open communications* - For readiness management, this involves establishing an open learning environment in which individuals are encouraged to assume responsibility and ownership for skills development.
- *Invest in quality* - Higher levels of productivity and quality require an investment in training and skills development within the organization.
- *Learn from all experiences* - On-going learning occurs not only in the classroom but also as a result of project experiences. By using milestone reviews and post-mortems, project teams are able to repeat successes by capturing best practices from prior project efforts.
- *Stay agile, expect change* - Individuals and project teams must be able to manage planned and unplanned change, especially in today's dynamic technological and economic environment.

Key Readiness Concepts

The following concepts are associated with the Readiness Management Discipline:

- *Understanding the experience you have* - Central to establishing a readiness management effort is knowledge assessment and management. One of the most vital assets of the organization is the collective knowledge and experiences of its human resources. Using this asset requires providing mechanisms for assessing and accessing individual knowledge.

- *Willingness to Learn* - In terms of readiness management, this concept is focused on knowledge acquisition and distribution as well as a personal commitment to continuous self-improvement.
- *Continuously managing readiness* - An essential element of proactive readiness management is incorporating training programs and other learning activities into project schedules.

Proven Readiness Practices

The following practices are associated with the Readiness Management Discipline:

- *Carry out readiness planning* - Effective readiness management requires advance planning and coordination in order to ensure availability of training resources as well as seamless integration with other project activities.
- *Measure and track skills and goals* - A vital activity associated with readiness management involves the assessment and tracking of individual skills and goals. The assessment function should ensure that current knowledge and abilities are measured along with desired capabilities.
- *Treat readiness gaps as risks* - Proficiency gaps should be identified as risks at the project level. Doing so allows the project team to identify appropriate mitigation strategies and contingency plans in advance.

The Readiness Management Process

The MSF Readiness Management Discipline defines a readiness management process that represents a continuous, proactive, and iterative approach to skills readiness, and that adapts well to projects of varying sizes and complexities. The readiness management process consists of four basic steps: *Define*, *Assess*, *Change*, and *Evaluate*, shown in figure 11.2. Each step is further composed of a series of tasks leading to the next step in the process.

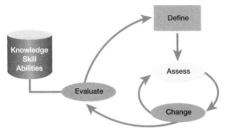

Figure 11.2 MSF Readiness Management Process Diagram

Readiness Definition

The first step of the readiness management process is 'Define', which involves identifying the level of knowledge, skills, and abilities needed by the project team. During this step, three components of readiness referred to as *Scenarios*, *Competencies*, and *Proficiencies* are addressed. The primary outputs of the readiness definition step include identified competencies with desired proficiency levels as well as competencies and proficiencies correlated with the appropriate scenario.

Scenarios

Scenarios describe the situation or context surrounding the introduction of new technology projects within an organization. Scenarios are classified as either *High Potential*, *Strategic*, *Key Operational*, or *Support*. These categories are loosely correlated with the phases and challenges associated with developing and managing technology products. Because each scenario involves different approaches for acquiring resources and skills, classifying IT projects by scenario type enables readiness planning to be performed based on the unique aspects of a given project.

Competencies

From a readiness perspective, competency refers to the knowledge, skills, and performance requirements needed in order to perform the tasks associated with a given IT scenario. Whereas knowledge describes the information a person must have to perform a job in a competent manner, skills describe the behaviors that comprise competency in a specific area. Performance requirements describe the expected outcome of a task or set of tasks for a particular job role assuming a proficient level of knowledge and skills.

Proficiencies

Proficiency is a measure of a person's ability to perform a set of tasks for a given IT scenario. The level of proficiency for a given competency, which is determined at the time of the assessment, is used to establish a benchmark for determining proficiency gaps between current skills and the skills necessary to complete tasks associated with a given project. Identified proficiency gaps are subsequently addressed though the creation and implementation of learning plans, which describe the actions for moving to targeted levels of proficiency.

Readiness Assessment

The second step of the readiness management process is 'Assess', which involves determining the current set of competencies for each member of the project team. Proficiency gaps are identified by comparing the set of assessed competencies to the desired set of competencies for each job role. Learning plans are developed to bridge proficiency gaps. The tasks performed during this step include: *Measure Knowledge, Skills, and Abilities; Analyze Gaps;* and *Create Learning Plans*. The primary output of the readiness assessment step is assessment output and gap analysis as well as learning plans.

Measure Knowledge, Skills, and Abilities

Assessments of individual competencies can be performed in one of two ways: self-assessment and skills assessment. The self-assessment option uses a series of questions to measure a person's perceived level of ability. By contrast, the skills assessment technique uses a variety of methods to measure the actual expertise of an individual.

Analyze Gaps

This task is focused on the analysis of proficiency gaps as determined through comparison of current-state performance levels to desired, future-state levels of performance.

Create Learning Plans

The output of the gap analysis activity is used to develop learning plans, which typically consist of formal and informal training activities. The learning plan describes a number of elements including required training materials, computer-based training (CBT) tools, on-the-job training assignments, and self-directed learning activities. A learning plan may also describe how learned information will be applied to job functions.

Readiness Change

The third step of MSF readiness management process is 'Change', which implements and executes the training activities defined in the learning plan. The tasks performed during this step include training and progress tracking. The primary output of the readiness change step is the knowledge gained from training activities as well as progress-tracking data.

Training

The training task includes those elements described in the learning plan. These activities involve formal training classes, mentoring, self-directed training, and computer-based training.

Tracking Progress

Tracking progress involves monitoring accomplishments and the status of learning plans. Tracking progress is an essential aspect of the readiness change step, since it enables the organization to assess individual and overall readiness, and incorporate changes to readiness plans.

Readiness Evaluation

The final step of the MSF readiness management process is 'Evaluate', which determines the efficacy of the overall readiness process as well as learning plans. The main goal of this step is to determine if the desired future state was attained as a result of the readiness change step. Readiness evaluation consists of two primary tasks: review results and manage knowledge. The outputs from the readiness evaluation step include feedback, certifications, and knowledge management systems.

Review Results

This task is concerned with determining the effectiveness of the knowledge transfer activity. Activities performed during this step include self-assessment of skills learned as well as certification.

Manage Knowledge

Knowledge gained through training and other learning activities not only helps the individual attain specific goals and objectives, but also contributes to the intellectual property of the organization. If properly managed, information that is acquired through implementation of learning plans can be re-used and shared, fostering a learning community. The MSF Readiness Management Discipline advocates the development of knowledge management systems to facilitate the transfer and sharing of proven practices and lessons learned, as well as create a skills baseline of the knowledge contained within the organization.

12. Project Management Discipline

Overview

Regardless of their size, complexity, or industry, all projects require a set of defined disciplines to be effectively managed and brought to a successful conclusion. Collectively, this set of knowledge, skills, tools, and techniques is referred to as the discipline of project management. The most widely accepted international organization that promotes the discipline of project management and certifies individuals in these competencies is the Project Management Institute (PMI). A set of generally accepted project management knowledge promoted by PMI is embodied in the Project Management Body of Knowledge (PMBoK) document, entitled *A Guide to the Project Management Body of Knowledge*. MSF recognizes and endorses the PMBoK, and the Project Management Discipline of MSF is closely aligned with the PMI. Inherent within the MSF Project Management Discipline are the nine knowledge areas of the PMBoK. It is, however, the execution of the discipline of project management through the Team and Process Models of MSF that provides for the unique application of this discipline for IT projects.

Characteristics of Project Management

Project Accountability and Responsibility

MSF draws a clear distinction between the authority of a project, or 'who is in charge', and the discipline of project management, the knowledge, skills, tools and techniques. While MSF attaches great importance to the discipline and competencies associated with project management, within the Team Model there is a notable absence of a specific role or job title called project manager. This may seem surprising for a framework that emphasizes project management principles. It is, however, an indication of how the principles of MSF lead to a project management approach where responsibility for project management is distributed to team leads and project management activities are performed by all team members. Separating the person from the activities allows MSF to have a distributed team approach to project management activities that improves accountability and allows for a great range of scalability from small projects up to very large, complex projects.

Five Project Characteristics

As the IT community searches to improve project delivery success, formal project management practices have been a source of great interest, while recognizing that traditional approaches to project management may have to be adjusted to meet the different characteristics of IT projects. In a recent study carried out by the Gartner Group, five project characteristics were highlighted as areas of difference between IT projects and those of other industries, shown in table 12.1.

Project Characteristic	Construction/Engineering	Information Technology
Change	Slow and incremental	Rapid and unplanned
Requirements	Explicit and documented	Ambiguous and vague
Roles	Specialists	Utility players
Implementation	Six Sigma	Controlled crisis
Budgeting/Scheduling	Historically based	Historically unfounded

Table 12.1 Differences in IT Projects from Construction/Engineering Projects

The MSF Project Management Discipline addresses the differences in the project characteristics highlighted in this study. It does this through the application of the different activities of the discipline across the team. By recognizing that all the project management activities are essential but not embodied in a single role or person, it increases total team commitment to project management.

Project Manager or Program Manager

Although MSF does not use the term 'project manager' to describe someone who is a specialist in project management, the MSF Program Management role places the greatest emphasis on the

Project Management Discipline. This role most closely resembles the traditional project manager role in focus and responsibility. An MSF team, however, is structured as a team of peers. In this model, the Program Management role takes a highly facilitative approach to performing the functions within its responsibilities. As such, the MSF team would organizationally be structured similar to cross-functional teams in a matrix organization. These are multi-disciplinary teams that combine the skills and focuses from different areas of the organization into a single team assembled for the project.

Additionally, the MSF team structure and Project Management Discipline allow projects to have a team where the Program Management role is not filled by someone who has organizational authority over other members of the team. Under this structure the authority and decision-making clout of any individual on the team is based on their contribution to the project success and not on their title or organizational position.

Effective Teams
This approach to distributing, or more precisely, sharing the project management skills and responsibilities across the team has proven to be the most effective team structure for the highly creative and constantly changing environment in which IT projects operate.
It also capitalizes on the highly independent nature of the IT work-force. Within this type of a team, leadership is emphasized over management, and the role of Program Management owns greater responsibility for leading through a shared vision, through clear communications, responsibility, and accountability. Program Management uses facilitation and coaching, rather than attempting to impose control on the rest of the team.

Two key elements are necessary for distributed project management to work within a team of peers. These are a shared vision of the solution and an effective team environment based on trust and mutual accountability. Without these two base elements, the separation of responsibilities into roles with no single control point for decision-making and organizational management can lead to the team quickly degrading into a dysfunctional state, which is evidenced by multiple agendas and anarchy.

Principles of Successful Project Management

The MSF Project Management Discipline is built on the principles of MSF. It is easy to relate these principles to the activities and competencies necessary to perform effective project management of IT projects through a few examples.

- The application of certain control processes involving scope and change management requires *open communications, staying agile*, and *expecting change* while *establishing clear accountability*.
- Leading teams to a *shared vision* that focuses on providing meaningful *business value* while *investing in quality* requires project management practices that *empower teams*.
- Facilitating milestone reviews fosters a *continual learning experience*, and improves morale through frank and *open communications*. Both are focused on *investing in quality*.

Project Management through the Project Life Cycle

The focus on the discipline of Project Management through the development of these skills and competencies for all team members is essential to improving the chances of project success. The MSF Team Model provides some level of specialization within the team by creating roles that focus on the different aspects of success for the project. By doing this, the core concepts of the PMBoK, (the nine knowledge areas itemized in table 12.2) are shared across the team roles, throughout the project life cycle.

Like the other MSF Disciplines of Risk and Readiness Management,

Project Management is continually exercised throughout the entire project life cycle. Some project management knowledge areas will naturally be more prevalent during certain phases of the project. Table 12.2 indicates how the PMBoK knowledge areas intersect with the MSF Process Model phases, whether on an application development or on an IT infrastructure deployment project. Phases may have greater or lesser emphasis on each of the nine knowledge areas as indicated by a primary or secondary designation.

Project Management Knowledge Area	Envisioning	Planning	Developing	Stabilizing	Deploying
Integration Management	S	P	P	S	P
Scope Management	P	P	S	S	S
Time Management	S	P	P	S	P
Cost Management	S	P	P	S	P
Quality Management	S	P	P	P	P
Human Resource Management	S	P	P	S	S
Communications Management	P	P	P	P	P
Risk Management	P	P	P	P	P
Procurement Management	S	P	P	P	S

Table 12.2 Knowledge Areas of PMBoK by MSF Process Model Phase
(P indicates a primary emphasis and S indicates a secondary emphasis)

As the project progresses through the phases of the life cycle, the on-going project management practices of planning, estimating, and scheduling, along with the control processes of risk management, scope management and quality management are performed as often as necessary to effectively manage the success of the project.

Project Management Responsibilities and Dealing with Scalability

MSF provides a scalable way to ensure that project management functions are met from the very smallest projects up to very large or complex projects. This approach prevents excessive bureaucracy in smaller projects while providing sufficient management structure for larger, more complex ones. In further examination of the MSF approach to project management within the framework of the MSF Team Model, three distinctive attributes stand out. These are:

- Most of the responsibilities of the role commonly known as 'project manager' are encompassed in the MSF Program Management role cluster, as previously explained.
- In larger projects requiring scaled-up MSF teams, project management activities occur at multiple levels.
- Some large or complex projects require a specialist project manager or project management team.

Small Projects

In small projects, all the functional project management responsibilities are typically handled by a single person filling the Program Management role cluster. As the size and complexity of a project grows, this role cluster is broken out into two branches of specialization: one dealing with the management of the project deliverables and the other dealing with the management of the project environment and team. Exactly how project management is distributed depends in large part on the scale and complexity of the project.

Larger Projects

On larger projects with sub teams, the team lead is the point of integration with the rest of the larger team. Team leads have some project management responsibilities at the level of their sub team, filling the Program Management role for that sub team.

Complex Projects

As a project gets larger or more complex, it can become overwhelming to manage project artifacts, update schedules, coordinate team communications, manage control processes, track progress reporting, and perform other project management activities. To cope with this, it often makes sense to divide the responsibilities of the Program Management role cluster. Based on the skills available and the type of project, these activities and responsibilities can be divided across multiple people. One potential approach is to separate the role into a project administrator and a dedicated project manager.

Practices of Successful Project Management

At the heart of the Project Management Discipline is the desire and responsibility to maximize the productivity of the team so that it can effectively deliver on the expectations of the organization - the highest quality in the shortest time for the least cost. By focusing on productivity, and any efforts that will enhance productivity through project management practices, the team stands the best chance to deliver on these expectations.

Process Assurance

One of the primary activities of project management is process assurance. Having defined processes that are appropriate for their purpose and commonly understood by all provides the team with certainty of action, thus preventing recreation of standard artifacts or confusion about repeatable processes. Certain control processes, such as change management, risk management, and issue management will be ignored or difficult to manage if not defined and deliberately attended to. Performing the activities that encourage and support these processes, at the level appropriate for the project, is a sign of effectively distributed and valued project management on a team.

Project Structure

Tightly integrated with process assurance, and equally essential, is effective project structure. Project structure can be thought of as the formalization of the processes within the project environment. Structure creates the environment in which the project is conducted. Applied effectively, structure provides commonality and certainty within the team around the mechanics of the project: Who is responsible for what, where do things go, and how does information flow among team members. By creating a positive and well-understood environment, structure provides clarity to the team regarding daily activities and fosters mutually agreed-upon expectations.

Leadership and the Team Psyche

The third opportunity for improving productivity is in the area of team leadership. Leadership focuses on the team psyche. This is the collective interaction of the individuals on the team within the context of their processes and structure. Simply put, it's the combination of the thoughts, emotions, and behaviors of the team in response to its environment (process and structure). Most often, project management focuses on the hard and tangible skills of process assurance and structure, yet understate the importance of leadership and attendance to the team psyche. Left unattended, projects can degrade to a well administered but dysfunctional state. The MSF Project Management Discipline puts a heavy emphasis on leadership beyond the elements of process assurance and structure.

13. Implementing MSF

Using the Framework and Modular Structure

The MSF principles, the disciplines (Risk Management, Readiness Management, and Project Management), as well as the models (Team and Process) make up the complete framework.

Organizations seeking to deliver superior business results through the successful deployment of technology projects may use MSF in its entirety or in part by determining how the six components (see figure 1.1) will provide the greatest benefit given their culture, business needs, and most common reasons for project failures. MSF is easy-to-learn and easy-to-use; however, organizations, teams, and individuals need to evaluate if MSF is appropriate for them. This starts with assessing their:

- Readiness to understand and embrace MSF's principles.
- Openness to change coupled with the ability to garner executive sponsorship for that change.
- Ability to align their needs and desires with the direct and indirect goals of MSF.
- Challenges, shortcomings, and failures (do they resemble those MSF was designed to address?).

Teams can begin communicating and applying the MSF principles to projects immediately, to begin accruing benefits, and to assess readiness for moving to MSF. Whether the choice is to use individual MSF components or the entire framework, the approach is the same: learn as much as possible through white papers, training and guidance (mentoring and MSF-experienced leadership), then start small. Apply the MSF Team and Process Models to one or more relatively small projects. Incorporate the disciplines as necessary adding detail and depth with repetition. Get organizational sponsorship. Recognize and celebrate successes; proven results accelerate adoption and create sustainable change.

MSF and Capability Maturity Model Integration

IT organizations that recognize the role that process maturity plays in project failures often refer to and seek guidance from the Capability Maturity Model Integration (CMMI). The Software Engineering Institute (SEI) proposed the original framework with which software processes can be defined (SW-CMM) using five maturity levels. Within each level are key process areas that identify the required behaviors that must be present before an IT organization can advance to the next level of maturity. The overarching theme is that the greater the maturity of the process, the greater the project success rate and lower overall cost. The CMMI provides product and process improvement models by leveraging the best practices from the SW-CMM, the Systems Engineering Capability Model (SECM), and the Integrated Product Development Capability Maturity Model (IPD-CMM).

Both CMMI and MSF emphasize the importance of incremental and continuous improvement for software development and engineering processes where well-defined disciplines create the backbone of the process, and experience provides valuable learning. The focus for each is different, however. The MSF Process Model addresses the team's learning and experience while the Readiness Management Discipline supports the individual's learning and skills. CMMI's focus is organizational learning and recognition of what moves it toward greater process maturity. Both CMMI and MSF set forth best practices and processes to guide learning and to improve capabilities - there is some overlap, but there are also practices and process that are unique to each. Organizations wishing to increase their process maturity will find many benefits from MSF. Not only is it easy to digest and follow, its scalable structure makes it easy to use on small projects without getting sidelined into creating additional documentation or other overhead required by a process intended for large, complex projects.

Integrating MSF with other Project Management Approaches

MSF and the contemporary project management schools of thought represented by the Project Management Institute (PMI), the International Project Management Association (IPMA), and PRojects IN Controlled Environments (Prince2) are completely compatible - philosophically and structurally. These project management approaches have evolved from the more mature engineering and construction industries into internationally known and accepted standards applicable to the field of project management. The IT industry has tended to be dynamic and less formal than older organizations. This industry has been challenged to apply the general set of disciplines and techniques to development and infrastructure projects. MSF responds to this need by focusing specifically on the unique aspects of IT. Because MSF is built on the same core set of disciplines used across the project management field, organizations that use traditional project management or follow a specific methodology can use MSF and integrate it into their organizations and projects.

Just as MSF emphasizes the importance of distinct project team roles and a Process Model that can be used iteratively to progressively define, develop, test, and implement a project, traditional project management provides guidance for defining and assigning project roles and responsibilities and allows for either a spiral (iterative) or waterfall life cycle. The underlying philosophy for both is that IT projects must practice universal Project Management Disciplines to effectively deliver on project commitments. Each approach has its own strengths:

- The Project Management Body of Knowledge (PMBoK) provides generic project management guidance with broad application across industries.
- MSF's domain is Information Technology and the numerous challenges unique to software and systems development.

Overall, when MSF's Process and Team Models are combined with the disciplines of Risk, Readiness and Project Management, MSF can be viewed as fully compliant with PMBoK's life cycle process. MSF's relationship to a larger knowledge base, the Microsoft Enterprise Services Framework, extends MSF beyond project management. By connecting MSF to an overarching framework that includes MOF and Microsoft Enterprise Architecture, MSF is part of a holistic approach for managing people, process, and technology. The focus of this approach is on enabling IT to dramatically increase project successes and continuously improve its support of business success.

Project teams that plan to blend MSF with a specific methodology should discuss, explicitly, how the two will be integrated and applied. Since organizations and projects vary widely in their size, complexity, and resources, the melding of the two will always be unique. Recognizing the need to maximize team performance while achieving the project's goals will facilitate this discussion.

Also, consider using the outline of the methodology to construct points of comparison and integration with MSF. For example, MSF and PMBoK can be integrated by correlating the five PMBoK process groups (Initiating, Planning, Executing, Controlling and Closing) and MSF process areas (Envisioning, Planning, Developing, Stabilizing, Deploying) with each other. Additionally, this exercise will show that the MSF Process Model covers all of the nine PMBoK knowledge areas (using different terminology). The integration of the two approaches should be discussed at length and agreed upon.

MSF and Agile Principles

MSF and Agile software methodologies such as eXtreme Programming (XP) and Adaptive Software Development share a common heritage of software engineering that incorporates many of the same sound principles. These leading-edge approaches embrace similar characteristics or best practices, some of which include:

- Team-oriented.
- Change-oriented.
- Customer collaboration.
- Requirements-driven design and development.
- Component-based architecture.
- Iterative development.
- Adaptability.

Recognizing that no software process can be considered complete due to the constantly changing and chaotic landscape of IT, each of these approaches continues to evolve, making significant investments in their process and/or framework product. Detailed comparisons to MSF, then, may become outdated by new releases of these other products. At a summary level, however, MSF can be said to be compatible with Agile methodologies and provide additional benefits when used to augment them.

Agile Methodologies and MSF

Agile methodologies place emphasis on *software development* and practices that apply primarily to design and development phases whereas MSF is applicable to *all types of IT projects*. The Agile methodologies align closely with MSF's principle-based approach and best practices striking a balance between the need for structure and flexibility. In combining the two, MSF's structured framework supports a repeatable process that can be scaled to projects of different sizes and complexity, in concert with Agile methods for development.

Integration with MSF

IT organizations that have already implemented Agile methodologies may choose to extend them by adding MSF. The main advantage of this combined approach is to build a consistent framework that applies both to software development projects and other types of IT projects. Since Agile Methodologies tend to be centered on software development efforts, MSF may be used to round out an organization's ability to manage IT projects by providing a standard approach to use not only on software development, but also on infrastructure, and enterprise software integration projects. MSF provides a comprehensive method for meeting solution delivery and deployment objectives, and supplements this with MOF guidance to achieve operational excellence.

Organizations that are considering MSF or Agile methodologies for the first time should follow the recommended training curriculum and (incremental) implementation of MSF to help establish an appreciation for using a defined project process. This should facilitate the acceptance and perceived value of a more procedural process.

Tips and Considerations

Microsoft recognizes there are many challenges that must be dealt with when implementing MSF or any project process approach for the first time. The organization or company culture, its openness to change, the background, experience, and skills of the team members must all be taken into account. Since MSF looks at the business and IT as a whole, it's important to help customers as well as IT development, infrastructure, integration, and operations staff recognize the benefits of using MSF. Identifying the factors that contribute to project successes and failures within the organization and/or business is an appropriate starting point as it promotes a common understanding and rationale for change across the organization.

This pocket guide outlines some of the common reasons for failure, which may be used to open this dialogue between the business and IT. Additional information on the causes of technology project failures and how MSF can be used to better meet business objectives and implement technology is readily available through numerous channels. Microsoft offers a collection of white papers, training materials and courses, mentoring, and project leadership to introduce people to MSF and build their competencies in using it.

For more help, a list of resources is included in the Additional Information chapter of this guide.

14. Additional Information

Information on MSF and MOF

MSF offers guidance through online MSF white papers, training and certification, consulting services by MSF Practitioners, and a wide range of templates, tools, and techniques. For specific technology scenarios and guidance in the application of MSF and Microsoft technologies, there are additional courses, product documentation, TechNet and MSDN articles, as well as Microsoft service offerings and solution accelerators.

Information about MSF can be obtained from the Microsoft Solutions Framework Web site (within the MSF Resource Library) on TechNet at http://www.microsoft.com/msf. There are currently over 600 MSF Practitioners trained on version 3.0; for a list of endorsed MSF Practitioners, contact estrain@microsoft.com.

Information about MOF can be obtained from the Microsoft Operations Framework Web site on TechNet at http://www.microsoft.com/mof. The MSF pocket guide was based upon the white papers version 3.0. Also, the *MOF Pocket Guide* provides a practical reference to MOF.

References

Microsoft Solutions Framework Essentials courseware for Course 1846A, 2002, Microsoft Corporation.

Data sheets for MSF version 3.0 and the Practitioner Program, 2003, Microsoft Corporation, available at http://www.microsoft.com/msf.

Microsoft Solutions Framework white papers, available through the MSF Resource Library at http://www.microsoft.com/msf:

- *MSF Version 3.0 Overview*, 2003, Microsoft Corporation.
- *MSF Team Model v.3.1*, 2002, Microsoft Corporation.
- *MSF Process Model v.3.1*, 2002, Microsoft Corporation.
- *MSF Risk Management Discipline v.1.1*, 2002, Microsoft Corporation.
- *MSF Readiness Management Discipline v.1.1*, 2002, Microsoft Corporation.
- *MSF Project Management Discipline v.1.1*, 2002, Microsoft Corporation.

15. Acronyms and Glossary

Definitions are taken directly from the *Microsoft Solutions Framework Essentials* courseware unless otherwise indicated.

Baseline	A measurement or known state by which something is measured or compared, which is necessary for managing change. It can be thought of as a snapshot at a set point in time.
Bug	Any issue arising from the use of the solution.
Build	A periodic assembly of all the solution elements that is sufficiently complete to be included in the build. Builds include code components, directory structures, infrastructure elements, documentation, and sometimes automated deployment scripts.
Constraint	A nonfunctional requirement that applies to various aspects of projects (such as budget, resources, technology, and so on) and that places a limit or dictates a limited range of possibilities.
Customer	An individual or organization that expects to gain business value from the solution and is the recipient of a service or product.
Deliverable	A physical artifact created by the team, usually associated with reaching an interim or major milestone.
Discipline	In MSF, a discipline is a set of industry processes and best practices as represented in the Risk Management, Readiness Management, and Project Management Disciplines.
Environment	A collection of hardware, software, network communications, and procedures that work together to provide a discrete type of computer service.
Enterprise Architecture	A structure that describes: the organization's business activities; the applications and automation that support those business activities; the information necessary to carry out those business activities; and, the technologies and infrastructure used to deliver the applications and information.
Framework	A structure or frame designed to support something - it is assembled of component parts that integrate and fit together.
IT	Information Technology. Includes information systems and technology organizations.
ITIL	Information Technology Infrastructure Library
IT Life Cycle	The phases a solution goes through from the time it is conceived until the time it is retired from service.
ITSM	Information Technology Service Management
Living Document	A document that is regularly updated and referred to.

Milestone	A point on the project schedule at which the project team assesses progress and quality, and reviews deviations in scope and specifications. A project may use numerous milestones, external (or major) and internal (or interim).
MOF	Microsoft Operations Framework
MSF	Microsoft Solutions Framework
Model	A schematic or graphical representation of principles, concepts, and best practices that describe an entity or process. The two MSF models are Team and Process.
PMBoK	Project Management Body of Knowledge
PMI	Project Management Institute
Process	A coherent sequence of activities that yield a result, product, or service; usually a continuous operation. A series of actions or operations designed to achieve an end.
Process Model	A high-level sequence of activities for building and deploying IT solutions. *[source: MSF Process Model v.3.1]*
Project	A temporary endeavor undertaken to create a unique solution, service, or result.
Project life cycle	A collection of generally sequential project phases whose name and number are controlled by the needs of the organization or organizations involved in the project.
Proven practices	A procedure or functional principle that, based on industry experience, is considered by experts to be optimal (may be termed 'proven best practices').
Release	A collection of new and/or changed configuration items that are tested and then introduced into the production IT environment.
Role cluster	A role cluster, also referred to as role, may be one or many people depending on the size and complexity of a project, as well as the skills required to fulfill the responsibilities of the functional areas. *[source: MSF Team Model v.3.1]*
Service	Since MSF and MOF intersect, it is important to note that MOF (IT operations) uses the term 'service' or 'service solution'. A 'service solution' is the capabilities that IT provides to the business, defined in terms of functionality at the user level.
Solution	Within MSF, the solution is the 'technical solution', the coordinated delivery of the elements needed to successfully respond to a customer's business problem or opportunity. A solution includes technologies, documentation, and training, as well as relevant aspects of service support and delivery (related to MOF) among others.
Sponsor	Individuals who initiate and approve a project and its results.
Stakeholder	A person with a significant interest in the outcome of a project. A business unit vice president is an example of a stakeholder.

Team Model	Microsoft's approach to structuring people and their activities to enable project success. The model defines role clusters, functional areas, responsibilities, and guidance for team members to address so that they can reach their unique goals in the project lifecycle. *[source: MSF Team Model v.3.1]*
User	The person who uses the solution or services on a day-to-day basis. Individuals or systems that directly interact with the solution.
Vision	An unbounded view of the solution.